Jerome Ocampo has taken brought it from just an am~~azing calling to individuals, to a~~ worldwide training movement. I believe this is preparing the way of the greatest explosion of a Jesus Movement the world has ever seen.

I'm so excited because in many ways this book and Jerome's life are helping my own dream come true. Before the return of Christ and the great day of the Lord, the Bible says that He would send the spirit of Elijah to turn the hearts of the fathers to the children and the children to their fathers. We dreamed that dream, we prayed that dream, and now that dream is being built through a book like this. Don't just read it, consecrate yourself, connect yourself to fathers and mothers or as fathers and mothers connect yourself to a son or daughter and bring forth this great awakening in the earth. Thank you, Jerome, for taking my story further than I ever could have myself.

Lou Engle, revivalist, visionary,
Co-founder of TheCall, Inc., Pasadena, California

Jerome Ocampo is the man whom God has raised for this hour to galvanize the Youth in Asia to bring them into the Nazarite Consecration. From the first time I met him, till today, he has been solid in his commitment and assignment. And whilst many others have deflected from the heavenly vision, not my friend, Jerome.

He is consumed with the burning desire to see Asia's youth burn with a fiery zeal for the Lord and His holiness and to this end, he plods on, tirelessly. His book, *The Rise of the Digital Nazarite* will ignite the hearts of the young among our ranks. I love this man and consider him to be a dear friend and trusted comrade.

Rev. Yang Tuck Yoong
Senior Pastor, Cornerstone Community Church Singapore
Director, Bible College of Wales, Swansea

God has made an information highway for such a time as this—for a generation with the passion and knowledge to change the face of the globe as Jesus Revolutionaries. Jerome Ocampo has written both the manifesto and training manual to train this army. I, for one, can't wait for the revival, awakening, and reformation that God is about to release across the face of the earth!

Cindy Jacobs, Generals International
Dallas, Texas

In 1984, I was a clueless, idealistic missionary, who was attempting to plant a student church in Manila's University Belt. Jerome Ocampo was one of the first Filipino pastors I met. He graciously welcomed my wife, Deborah, and me to his nation and encouraged us to do what we felt God called us to do. Because we were the same age, and we were both products of the Jesus Movement, we hit it off immediately.

Jerome's passion for Jesus, his commitment to social responsibility, and his calling to university students is as strong today as when I first met him over three decades ago. I pray the global Church will hear and heed the voice of God through my friend Jerome.

Pastor Steve Murrell, Cofounder/President—Every Nation
Pastor—Victory in Manila, Philippines

Rise of the Digital Nazarites is a must read for those of us intent on giving our lives for the next generation. Jerome is spot on in his first book regarding the perils and needs of today's millennials. The potential of a fresh global outpouring of the Holy Spirit is before us but it will require an unprecedented intergenerational unity as spiritual fathers and mothers and spiritual sons and daughters turn their hearts toward one another. New generations are crying for this kind of unity, and when it is realized, we will witness a release of blessing that will shake the world. So, let us soften our hearts and seize this moment to raise up a new army of Digital Nazarites who will carry the mantel of Spirit-empowered Christianity to the ends of the earth. This is our Day!

Billy Wilson, President, Oral Roberts University
Empowered21
Tulsa, Oklahoma

I have come to know Pastor Jerome Ocampo as one of the most prominent in rank leaders with inspiring the millennials and youth of all ages to dream bigger than themselves. In his book the *Rise of the Digital Nazarites* he stimulates us, the old and the young, out of boredom and out of mediocrity. He challenges the youth out of wholeness in the midst of a spiritually polluted environment of pornography and Godlessness. The digital Nazarite Movement starts with awakening their extreme lifestyles that can inspire their generation to purpose. Pastor Jerome shares the global attacks on this generation. He uses the biblical prophet Elijah as an example of how the elders of this generation must be a model for the next.

Rise of the Digital Nazarites is one of many books to come out of Jerome Ocampo's anointed assignment from God. His book brings the old generation alongside the new; his desire is for the new generation to stand on the shoulders of spiritual fathers who have not bowed their knee to belial. He inspires the old generation to dream their dreams so that youth may birth their visions standing on their spiritual shoulders. Pastor Jerome has set forth the strategy that all those dealing with youth should take heed.

As one who has written books and understands how important it is to bring the hearts of the fathers back to the children and the children to the fathers, I recommend including this much needed guide in your library.

Al Hollingsworth, Coach,
Founder of B.O.S.S. The Movement Global Ministries
Ontario, California, United States

RISE OF THE DIGITAL NAZARITES

WHEN
THE
MILLENNIAL
GENERATION
DISCOVERS THE
ANCIENT
PATH

JEROME OCAMPO

Published by:
R. H. PUBLISHING
3411 Preston Road Ste. C-13-146
Frisco, Texas 75034

Copyright © 2017, Jerome Ocampo

ISBN#978-0-9976907-7-4 (paperback)
ISBN#978-0-9976907-9-8 (ebook)

ACKNOWLEDGMENTS

I want to thank my wife, Annabelle (Abel) Ocampo, who kept on pushing me to finish this book. She continuously inspired me and persistently challenged me to put everything into writing. She was with me in all my journeys mentioned in this book and was my main partner with the vision.

I want to thank Lou Engle, who opened my eyes to the vision and passion for prayer. I thank Cindy Jacobs for always being an encouragement, prophesying that I will write this book. She has been a friend to my family and to my nation.

I want to thank Attorney Philip Yotoko and Attorney Randy Patton for helping me edit the manuscript and being the very first ones to read and honestly comment on this book. I thank my JREV staff, Mutya and Ziggie, who are my armor bearers throughout my journey.

I want to acknowledge my awesome church, from our leaders, Pastor Erich Santos and his wife, Miriam, for humbly recognizing my call to the nations, even when at times it was a sacrifice for our church, and for Minette Carag, who stood as our church's prophetic voice when needed.

I also thank our church, Jesus Flock Family, who walked me through the many challenges we faced in order to minister to the next generation.

Finally, I want thank my sons: Paul who led worship in all the JREV events, starting as young as 15 years old; Johan who never failed to encourage us in pursuing JREV and for Jemuel, who is always excited for the new things of God. JREV was birthed as an answer to our cry for our own boys—to keep them on fire for God.

And I will always sing to Jesus, "All is for your glory, all is for your Name."

FOREWORD

The call of the Nazarite has been the foundational message from which the ministry The Call has sprung. The Call has gathered hundreds of thousands from two generations to gather together to fast and pray for historic revival and awakening. In the 1990's I was privileged to speak with a movement called Rock the Nations. We traveled across America, calling young people to consecrate themselves to fast and pray so that America would turn back to God. That call to consecration and fasting was embodied in the Old Testament picture of the Nazarite. These men and women made a voluntary vow of consecration, and God used that vow to stem the tide of apostasy in Israel and to bring forth a fresh manifestation of God to the nation.

As we preached this message, God sent fire on it. We prophesied that the Nazarites were going to the National Mall in Washington, D.C., and when they would gather, it would be a sign that America was turning back to God. On September 2, 2000, four hundred thousand people came. An extreme fasting and praying young generation connected with fathers and mothers for twelve hours to fast and pray. It began the ministry of The Call. It has impacted the earth.

Seven months before The Call, at age thirteen, my own son, Jesse, came to me and said, "I want to be a Nazarite to The Call. I don't want to cut my hair for 7 months." He said, "I want to do a 40 day fast on juice. I don't want to play baseball this year, either. All I want to do is pray with you, Dad, for revival in America." I didn't know what to tell the young man, but at four o'clock in the morning, I was awakened by the voice of the Lord saying, "America is receiving her apostles, prophets and evangelists, but it has not yet seen her Nazarites."

I awoke with a jolt, and I knew that God was giving hope for a nation because he was going to raise up young men and women with old men and women, running together to create a revolution that would change nations. It happened. I saw it with my own eyes. After the great gathering in Washington, D.C., I traveled to the Philippines to speak in a conference where I shared the vision of the Call. I gave the very first VHS unedited version of TheCall Video to Jerome Ocampo. He was so stirred by the message that he decided to start a revolution, a Jesus Revolution. He released the word and bones started rattling. One hundred and fifty thousand plus people gathered to fast and pray in Manila. It started a Nazarite movement with solemn assemblies being filled with fasting and praying where two generations running together shook the islands.

It then took a leap over to Southeast Asia, and the message has not stopped running. In fact, in many ways, Jerome Ocampo has taken the message of the Nazarite and brought it from just an amazing calling to individuals, to a worldwide training movement. I believe this is preparing the way of the greatest explosion of a Jesus Movement the world has ever seen.

John the Baptist was the prototype Nazarite. He would not drink wine because he was to be filled with the Holy Spirit from birth. His calling is found in Luke 1:17 "… and he will go on before the Lord in the spirit and power of Elijah to turn the hearts of the fathers to the children and the children to their fathers …" It was this promise that would prepare the way for the Fathers double portion, Son Jesus.

It is my conviction that a consecrated generation connected to the fathers is being prepared worldwide to bring in a manifestation of Jesus, the Son of God. He manifests Himself through millions of sons and daughters, who have been fathered in the Father's house. They have been fasting and praying with consecrated love and will become the great voice, roaring in the nations of the earth.

I'm so excited because in many ways this book and Jerome's life are helping my own dream come true. Before the return of Christ and the great day of the Lord, the Bible says that He would send the spirit of Elijah to turn the hearts of the fathers to the children and the children to their fathers. We dreamed that dream, we prayed that dream, and now that dream is being built through a book like this. Don't just read it, consecrate yourself, connect yourself to fathers and mothers or as fathers and mothers connect yourself to a son or daughter and bring forth this great awakening in the earth. Thank you, Jerome, for taking my story further than I ever could have myself.

Lou Engle, revivalist, visionary,
Co-founder of TheCall, Inc., Pasadena, California

There are many people using phrases like "Fathering a generation" today. This often used expression sometimes comes with the concept of joining and understanding the generations, but Jerome Ocampo has actually reached across the gap in a compassionate way.

This is why he is the one to write a book boldly entitled, *Rise of the Digital Nazarites*. His roots are deeply imbedded in the past move of God that I was a part of myself. In fact, we had what we called "The God Squad" on my college campus, and we lived, ate, and were passionate for saving souls! We were Jesus Freaks, Jesus People and Jesus Revolutionaries!

I personally believe that this kind of passion can be transmitted. Mike and I have known Jerome for many years, and he is purely the epitome of the Jesus People. He burns with a fresh fire to see the generations fulfilling God's purpose together.

It takes quite a bit of courage to stay on the front lines. While he writes about the great causes that he has spear-headed, such as The Call Philippines and Uprising, I know a bit of the "behind the curtain" stress he has gone through to do such history-making events. Jerome has paid the price to be a voice crying in the wilderness, speaking to a forerunner generation.

I have heard him present some of the material in this revolutionary book. Each time I am touched and awed by his intelligent passion. He champions a generation that some of my own have written off as lazy and entitled. I thoroughly agree that the Millennials are waiting for a cause to believe in, and rather than marginalize them, we need to say to them, "Stand on my shoulders, let my ceiling be your floor!"

In fact, most leaders I know feel exactly that way. This book, *Rise of the Digital Nazarites* gives us language to express our heart cry.

Millennials, this is a book for you. I know it will challenge you as it did me. As I read the chapters, I personally searched my own heart and life, asking myself if I am walking in humility and holiness. I, personally, have taken a Nazarite vow of holiness and purity. On a personal note, I do not drink wine because of that calling. You might not choose that part of the calling. However, with all kinds of addictions beating on the door of your generation, you might choose this way of being counter-cultural.

Jerome is right when he says we are in an epic battle! We, as Nazarites, are swimming upstream and will have many Mt. Carmel-type confrontations with a desensitized culture. Reading this book will peel away any layers of compromise you might have acquired by being barraged on every side by a society that has thrust God out of its conversation.

God has made an information highway for such a time as this—for a generation with the passion and knowledge to change the face of the globe as Jesus Revolutionaries. Jerome Ocampo has written both the manifesto and training manual to train this army. I, for one, can't wait for the revival, awakening, and reformation that God is about to release across the face of the earth!

Cindy Jacobs
Generals International
Dallas, Texas

TABLE OF CONTENTS

PART 3—THE ANCIENT PATH REDISCOVERED

PART 4—THE CHOICE

PART 5—THE EPIC BATTLE

INTRODUCTION

This book is an answer to the many requests people have made from all over the world. Friends have asked, "Why not write a book about what you have always been speaking about: The Next Generation? And even though I have contemplated writing it for years, time flew by so fast that I now realize it has been more than 10 years since I started on this journey of understanding the next generation. A whole new generation is emerging—one that has never known our beginnings, one that has never been stirred or challenged, and potentially one we might lose.

It is a difficult task to write about generations and their purposes. I am both inadequate and incapable of bringing a comprehensive and sociologically complete research study on this subject, and I never intend to. I simply want to present my encounters and the impressions left in me about this present day "young generation," while continuously learning more about them.

I invite you to take a step back and look at the bigger picture. Many times when we stand too close, like standing in front of a six foot wall, it seems too high. But when you take a step backward, it does not look as high as it did up close. So, I invite you to step back and see for yourself.

You might have a son or a daughter who is part of this emerging generation. You may even be wondering, "Will I ever understand them?" Or maybe you are in an office surrounded by young emerging professionals who totally think differently than you do. They work more efficiently and learn faster with multitasking skills—like they have two or three brains.

A youth leader will face many difficult challenges with a generation who can be too sensitive about how they are treated, yet numb to what society in general goes through. We all have our encounters with this young bunch of highly visual, entertainment-hungry and computer-savvy creatures. We sometimes ask ourselves, "Where in the world did they come from?" It turns out they might be more connected with the world and its developments than we in the older generation are, and we might actually be the ones who are out of touch.

This book will bring us down to earth to see them for who they are. We will encounter them again in this book, but with the "one step backward" perspective. Many times while reading this book, you may have "hmmm" or "wow" moments. You will find yourself nodding several times and thinking that now I understand a little bit about my son or daughter. This can better help you work with them and mentor them in the right direction. When you start to focus your life on raising them up, then you might find you yourself have the spirit and power of Elijah.

I will use this phrase often in this book: The Spirit and Power of Elijah. It refers to God's prophecy in Malachi 4:5-6. God sends Elijah the prophet in the last days to "turn the hearts of the fathers to the sons and the heart of the sons to the fathers." This ability to turn our hearts in either way is what I refer to as the Spirit and Power of Elijah. You will see later on that there are three Elijah's mentioned in the Bible and that all of them have a significant role for the next generation.

However, maybe you are the "young creature" yourself, trying to find your significance in a very confusing world. I have read that your generation is one of the most stressed-out generations in history. It is like when a computer gets an overload of functions and memory, it hangs. The only way to fix it is to reboot it. Maybe this book can help you reboot, and in doing so you'll find your purpose and destiny in the process. If that happens then I would have fulfilled one of the purposes for this writing.

Maybe as you understand yourself, you will start to understand your parents or those in the "older world." It might dawn on you that your destiny is connected with theirs. While going through this book you might be drawn to them, either generally or personally, to your parents or your mentors. Either way, you might experience the Spirit and Power of Elijah coming to you, "turning your hearts" to the older generation.

The uniqueness of this young generation and the stabilizing strength of the old; the huge capacity of the young and the keen ability to focus of the old; the calling of the young to change the world and the destiny of the old to prepare them— all these will be highlighted in this book.

So whichever perspective you are coming from, this book will touch you and hopefully lead you to a choice. Let the Spirit and Power of Elijah come and be released as you read.

PART 1

THE POTENTIAL OF MILLENNIALS

Chapter 1

MY JOURNEY STARTED WITH AN AWAKENING ENCOUNTER

(4 a.m. in the Manila Hotel.)

I barely slept the whole night because of the huge preparations I made for the largest event I had ever spearheaded in my life. Many things were running through my mind. I walked to the park where the final sound checks were being made. I had been asked two weeks before why we were starting at 5 a.m., when most religious events at the park usually begin in the afternoon. Others had predicted or warned us that very few people would show up at 5 am. I had boldly declared that we would start whether we have 50 or 500.

As I approached the stage, I heard a roar of 50 thousand (police estimated) people at the Luneta Grandstand in Rizal Park, the biggest park in the Philippines. Our team ran to me to say they couldn't stop the crowd from worshipping, even when the worship team was just sound checking the system. Some police officers that walked the perimeter testified as to being so overwhelmed by the atmosphere of tears from the crowd that they started crying themselves. Later, our videographers reported that at a particular segment when we were washing the feet of the young people that they started to weep.

Toward the afternoon, 150 thousand people, young and old, had come from all the major island groups of the Philippines and from every major Christian denomination to fast and pray for the nation—starting at 5:00 in the morning to 9:00 in the evening. Jesus Revolution Now was born on November 30, 2001. This is a significant day indeed, as it is officially our National Heroes Day.

This journey had started when Che Ahn and Lou Engle came to the Philippines right after The Call DC in September 2000. They had gathered more than 400 thousand people in Washington, D.C. to fast and pray for America. Once I heard them, I knew in my heart my journey had begun. I thought that it would end on the day we gathered our nation for prayer. Little did I realize that the revolution was just beginning.

In the Philippines, the term *People Power Revolution* was coined after 5 million people marched the streets to stand up against a 25-year-old dictatorship (1986). The people wanted change, for they had had enough. Yet, after a new government, a revised constitution and even a free press, corruption continued to bury our nation in debt. After 14 years, a second People Power Revolution took place where 1.8 million people marched the streets of Manila to ask for the resignation of our then president (2001).

In the midst of the two People Power Revolutions, Jesus Revolution Now was birthed with 150 thousand people praying for change. I do not discount what the two peaceful People Power revolutions did to shift the direction of our nation, but many realized that it wasn't enough to root out a culture of corruption. A different kind of revolution was needed to transform our nation and end corruption—one that affects our culture—at the very heart of a people. As a frustrated nation, after two political but peaceful revolutions, God was preparing a different kind of revolution.

Jesus Revolution Now was a success on its first day. We thought it ended there. In fact, we donated the entire financial surplus to other ministries, thinking that it was not meant to be kept but given away. However, the revolution continued and every major city in the Philippines wanted to do a Jesus Revolution Now solemn assembly. I was sucked into a movement that had a life of its own.

At first I thought that many wanted a piece of that Luneta Park success. What was fueling this movement? Was it the sad state our nation was in where the majority of our people are suffering in poverty because of the systemic corruption? Was it the desperate cry for change? Maybe because our people were suffering and a genuine change could bring hope. Some even insinuated that it was the next American imported religious fad that everyone wanted to be a part of.

None of these could answer the question, "Why was there a continuous clamor for a movement for change? And then the movement started to spread to other nations. To my surprise, I was invited to speak over and over again in western nations where there is affluence and relatively nice living conditions. Places where social security is at its best; where people are given equal opportunity and corruption is at its lowest. Then it dawned on me. The movement is anchored in the DNA of this present generation. The Generation in every nation has the same DNA, and regardless of what the social conditions are, the emerging young people will seek to bring change.

This is a generation who is called and designed by God to be catalysts; a generation where revolution (sudden change) is at its core DNA. I believe God has been waiting for a generation like this, or should I say God has been intentionally raising up a generation for such a time as this.

Let me talk to you about a very DIFFERENT GENERATION today, one that has a unique assignment.

All over the world we see more and more the YOUNG breaking away from the accepted norms in order to bring CHANGE. This obvious restlessness comes from a generation that has the capacity to do a lot, but has been challenged to do so little. Even without saying it, they seem to ask the question, "Is there not a CAUSE big enough for me?"

Is it possible that God has been waiting for a generation like this—one that has a global and digital perspective; yet, is hungry for a reality that surpasses their regular media diet? Has God set this generation up to bring about the biggest, most talked about "revival and transformation" in the end times?

How we can "turn our hearts" to them? How do we raise them up in the "spirit and power of Elijah" as present day CATALYSTS?

Their driving force is change, their anointing is transformation, and their calling is revolution, God's kind!

It has been 16 years since the very first Jesus Revolution

Now in Luneta Park. As I have traveled in many places in the world, I have witnessed not only their potential for success, but also their chronic failure. I hope they pick up this book and read it.

Because I believe in them so much, I continue to pour out myself to these young Catalysts. The Psalmist spoke of them in chapter 24, verse 6,

"This is the generation of those who seek Him,
who seek Your face, O God of Jacob."

In this book, they will discover their DNA and thereby understand their DESTINY.

I also hope those who are my age will read this book, those who had a taste of revival or a glimpse of God visiting communities. The last Old Testament prophet mentioned that there would be a generation so hard to accept that we would need Elijah's powerful anointing to pursue them. He mentioned the need for TWO GENERATIONS synergizing, converging and thereby removing the curse of our nations. (Malachi 4:6). My goal is to change the way you look at the next generation. I hope to move you to live for their destiny.

It is time for a NEW REVOLUTION, not people power, but a JESUS REVOLUTION NOW, with a young emerging generation of Catalysts, working side by side with an aging generation of pioneers, who are hungry for a fresh move of God.

Chapter 2

FROM THE JESUS PEOPLE
TO THE JESUS REVOLUTION

"This is the generation of those who seek Him,
who seek your face, Oh God of Jacob."
Psalm 24:6

On June 21, 1971, the cover of *Time Magazine* read, "The Jesus Revolution." It aptly described the times I lived as a teenager. I became a Christian in the Jesus People Movement in 1975. At 15, I was radicalized, not by the communist movement in the university, but by a band of long-haired Jesus lovers who preached in the streets, played in a music band on top of a multi-colored bus, and lived in a community together in a big house called "Maranatha Center." It dramatically contrasted with the formal religious background I grew up in. I fell in love with the real Jesus.

During my last year of high school, this movement swept our campus. I led a small Bible study that started with 20 students, and in a few weeks, grew to more than 100. There was no strategy, no plan—just raw passion for God. The whole faculty in our school was shocked when we, our little Bible study group, being the top students in the campus voted against holding the prom night because we felt it was too worldly and a plain waste of money. I guess we didn't know any better. We were just so in love with this new found faith.

This love is so intense that I couldn't think of living without it for the rest of my life. I almost didn't go to college, just so I could establish a student center, preach on street corners, and play in a Christian Band, sharing His love to others. My co-disciples and I were passionate, determined and committed. This is what I thought was normal in the Christian life. Then I met the church institution, which was a big letdown.

They had more passion for the religious status quo than for Jesus. Commitment was very low, and no one dared rock the boat. We used to joke about it, "When I join the formal church, I need to backslide a bit in order to mix with them." What I experienced in the Jesus movement was indeed the normal Christian life, but it wasn't the common life lived in many churches.

This stirred us, (me and my co-disciples) to establish our own church. A bunch of teenagers establishing a radical, independent fellowship (we never used the term "church" as that connoted the old system) that sought to live a revolutionary life for Jesus. We called ourselves "The Jesus' Flock." We were inspired by Watchman Nee's Little Flock from China.

As a Pioneering church we established many ministries including a Christian School (Jesus Flock Academy), a rescue mission for street children and an orphanage. We held continuous community evangelistic meetings, marches for Jesus and sustained overnight prayer meetings. We organized summer mission trips, and at times, joined Open Doors with Brother Andrew to deliver Bibles to restricted countries.

You could find us on campuses, street corners and markets preaching, singing and worshipping. And yes, I met my partner in life and ministry, Abel, and yes, she is a woman. With her, our eyes on a great vision to serve God, we started our family with three sons, Paul, Johan and Jemuel. We call them our Shadrach, Meshach and Abednego. Life was good until … it didn't turn out like we envisioned it.

As expected the inevitable happened. Almost everyone in our ministry got married and had kids. Life caught up with us, and we ended up pursuing establishment of the institutions that we once avoided as radicals. Organization was not an option, it became a necessity. And the older we got the more comfortable we felt in working with the status quo.

Chapter 3

A GENERATION BORN TO BE CATALYSTS

Abel and I wondered why our children were not as passionate as we were when we were teenagers. We longed to see our teenage children live as we lived when we were in high school. But since they went to our very Jesus' Flock Academy what was there to change? It was our very own Christian school, established to raise up a generation of Christian leaders.

We saw our young sons and daughters go to the church we pioneered, attend the school we founded and live in our homes we built, but something was missing. They seemed subdued, unawakened and mediocre. It shocked me to think that we were unintentionally producing a generation that we avoided in our Jesus People days. Oh no! We just couldn't let that happen.

A friend of mine, who is an elder of a big church in Manila, once told me her concerns about her children. She said that when her kids were small, she dragged them to church. In Sunday school she would see them raise their hands. They were so cute then. But when her children became teenagers, she was shocked when her boys said, "Mom, we don't want to go to church anymore." And she couldn't do anything about it.

We were also alarmed at the increasing number of our very own high school graduates who were backsliding once they got into college. What was happening? Abel and I were having an awakening. You can't transfer passion for God through an institution. It has to be through a spiritual father and son/daughter transfer, from one generation to the next.

At that point, we met Lou Engle, who placed words into what we felt. He is as much a radical as our original disciplers, Bill and Lil Tinsley, who always found ways to share the Gospel through non-conventional ways. They were radical, passionate, bold and intense in their love for Jesus.

I took the challenge to call for a day to fast and pray for our nation to turn back to God—we called for a National solemn assembly. I believed it would restart a new Jesus People Movement, the way I remembered it to be. It would shake complacency, expose apathy and extinguish mediocrity. I thought we were doing a catalytic event for the next revival. Little did I realize that God was using it to awaken the sleeping DNA of a powerful generation of Catalysts.

"Can a Nation be born in one day?" was our battle cry. God could make our nation great one more time. In the 1960's, the Philippines was only second to Japan in prosperity. It was said that other nations looked at us with envy. We had the first Asian airlines, the best hotels and a booming economy. Then corruption set in, and our nation fell into debt. After two decades, our GDP ranking plummeted to second to the last nation in Asia.

A convergence of events and purpose collided. There was a cause, there was opportunity and there was a generation hidden. Their latent DNA would hear the sound of a trumpet blown. So our sons and daughters responded, and the challenge for change was music to their ears. Young people came in waves. Some have asked me, "How did you teach these young people to pray."

I replied, "I never did. I just 'unleashed' them!"

I understood they were different, but I couldn't put my finger on it until I saw it. They were unusual. They were not like my generation. They are a powerful generation meant to bring REVIVAL, REFORMATION AND REVOLUTION.

Chapter 4

THE MILLENNIAL GENERATION AND THE DIGITAL GENERATION

The world is changing very fast. In the Agricultural Age, significant cultural and social changes transpired in a generation. When the Industrial Age began, change happened in half a lifetime. But during this Information Age, change can potentially happen every three years or in some cases even every 28 days.

One of the most evident and distinctive marks of this generation is its ability to adapt to or embrace change. This is sometimes confused with tolerance, but in reality, the young generation is flexible or pliable enough for change.

I would describe this generation as a Digital Generation. Studies have shown that they are very dependent on digital tools. Although there are old-timers who can do well with computers (that's me), yet many get tired of the fast replacement of newer smart phones or software upgrades that have to be relearned every time. Why do they have to change the system if it still works? I guess the old saying is not as true today as it was, "If it ain't broken, then don't fix it." This generation will not fix it, but will upgrade it. Why is there a compulsion for upgrade? It's because we have a generation that is highly ADAPTABLE.

DEFINING THE MILLENNIAL GENERATION

Although many studies have presented that the Millennial Generation is older than the Digital Generation, it is the purpose of this book to try to understand the underlying motivations the present generation has.

People have pointed out to me that one generation is 40 years (the biblical measure for a generation). If you have your grandchildren with you, then you are relating to three generations. Obviously generations overlap.

In the context of Malachi 4:5-6, we see a different emphasis.

> "Behold, I am going to send you Elijah the prophet before the coming of the great and terrible day of the Lord. He will restore the hearts of the fathers to their children and the hearts of the children to their fathers, so that I will not come and smite the land with a curse."

Does God limit the interaction only between fathers and sons (2 generations) and intentionally omit the grandchildren (3rd generation)? I think we need to look at it from God's perspective and not from our technical definition of a generation.

I think the emphasis of this text is the "relationship" between the generations, rather than the identification of when a generation ends or begins. A Father and Son relationship is the focus, whether it is with a father and a grandchild or a young teenager with a boy. Let me explain.

When I visited a village in the Philippines to attend a funeral, I met a 5-year-old boy who was acting like a homosexual. He had lipstick on and full make up. I was surprised since the boy doesn't have hormones yet that can move him to have such a behavior. When I asked him how he started doing that, he told me that he has an 8-year-old friend who taught him. As you can see, an 8-year-old boy "fathered" a 5-year-old boy.

Malachi 4:5-6 focuses on a relationship pursued for Generational Transfer, not a technical definition of generations. You can look at it this way. A man doesn't have to be married in order to "father" a young disciple. A woman doesn't have to be a mother in order to "mother" a young woman in the ways of God. For example: John the Baptist, to whom the spirit and power of Elijah came upon, was single and there wasn't any indication that he had biological children, yet he fathered and prepared many for the Messiah.

This is why the Elijah that is to come is not just a literal person, but the "spirit and power of Elijah" as mentioned in Luke 1:17. It is the authority and the ability to father/mother the next generation.

MILLENNIALS TURN DIGITAL

But the challenge is that we have a very difficult and different generation. A study about Digitals provides a working understanding about how different they are.

Marc Prensky coined the term *digital native* in his work

"Digital Natives, Digital Immigrants," published in 2001. He concluded the following:

> "A **digital native** is a person who was born during or after the general introduction of digital technologies and through interacting with digital technology from an early age, has a greater comfort level using it. Alternatively, this term can describe people born during or after the 2000s, as the Digital Age began at that time; but in most cases, the term focuses on people who grew up with the technology that became prevalent in the latter part of the 20th century and continues to evolve today.

> "… The opposite of digital native is **digital immigrant**, an individual who was born before the existence of digital technology and adopted it to some extent later in life.

CONFLICTS BETWEEN GENERATIONS

> "Due to the obvious divide set between digital natives and digital immigrants, sometimes both generations are forced to meet which commonly results in conflicting ideologies of digital technology … With technology moving so fast it is hard for digital immigrants to keep up." (*Wikipedia, Digital Native*)

I would consider myself a Digital Immigrant. I used to

write all my messages on yellow paper or a notebook binder where I store on shelves. After more than 15 years of writing notes, how could I be comfortable with a laptop or even preach with an iPad? Even the way we conduct our Sunday schools has changed. Do you still remember Flannel Graphs? I was trained with flannel graphs. I am an expert in it.

Now Digitals have successfully combined videos with poetry, computers with communications and education with the social media. So whether you are a Digital Native or a Millennial who learned and became a Digital Immigrant, both belong to the same Digital Generation.

Chapter 5

EXTREME LIFESTYLE: THE DNA OF THE DIGITAL GENERATION

Winkie Pratney says about the teenagers of today,

"Once their mind is made up on something, they seem to be willing to go to the extreme for it. Their games, dress, language and life-style all reflect this **everything-or-nothing, go-for-it, there is no tomorrow attitude.**

"Once committed to a course, they appear to have **no reservation for self-preservation …**

"Digital culture has produced **digital perception**; there seems to be little sense of the gradual, the slow or the quietly growing. **Digitals often appear to have no volume control;** when they do things they do them either all-on or all-off.

"Digitals living in a post-modern culture that has **no boundaries and no lasting realities; they are hungry at heart** for a word that makes a difference, a message that is, in itself, a *Digital Message*—**a 'no compromise call' to holiness and truth.**"[1]

---

1. The Chapter on Ministering to the Youth, pp 64-73, Hosting the Holy Spirit, Che Ahn, published by Renew Books, CA., USA.

I believe God has waited a long time for such a people. Is God raising up a generation that will prepare for His greatest move on earth?

The characteristics of this generation point to the unique call they have. The attacks on them show them becoming victims or the collateral damage of the changes that the modern world is undergoing. The new kind of perspective they have has separated them from any other generation that has existed in our time. Are these mere coincidences or is God setting them up for something big? If so, they are not losers but God's Divine set up! God can turn them into a non-compromising, backboned, immovable generation of believers who live what they believe … I am seeing a rebirth of the Church in the Book of Acts. Or in my time, I'd say a new Jesus People Movement unlike any other!

Chapter 6

THE GLOBAL ATTACK ON THIS EMERGING GENERATION

The Digital Generation's Nightmare

Can you imagine your worst nightmare? Dealing with teenagers can be threatening for a youth pastor and   frightening for a young parent. I work with young people all the time, and so I am used to it. But when I had my own teenagers in my house, it was a different matter. Why? What's Wrong With Kids Today?

When my youngest son turned 21 he complained to us saying, "I don't understand teenagers today … what is wrong with them?" I was surprised at the comment since no one expects a generation gap between a 21-year-old and a 14-year-old. Although it seemed an exaggeration, I wondered how big the gap was between teenagers and me. I have no patience in learning the controls of a PlayStation or an Xbox.

Here are some unique characteristics of this generation, which no other generation had. (Headings are from www.moh. org/ leadership materials, entitled Digital Generation: Ministry at the Millennium age. I related it to my own experiences with young people.)

- OVER EXPOSURE TO MEDIA.

  There is no other generation that has had more exposure to media than this generation. In many places in the world, Media continues to impact the thinking of this generation on a 24/7 basis. No other generation has the same exposure as this. I still remember black and white TV and phones with cords and snail mail where you put letters in envelopes and you stuck a stamp on them. I remember fax machines to send documents to other countries. None of that is relevant today as emails move documents back and forth in real time. It is easy to understand that young people today think differently from the older generation. They are living in a new world, one that we only dreamed of when we were young. They are not the misfits in this world that many of us are.

- NO SENSE OF VISION.

  It has been perceived that this generation generally lived in a peaceful environment. Even if abortions continue, and although child trafficking and child abuse are all on the rise, we see a generation that seems to be insensitive to these. Because of this, many have thought that this is a generation without any dream or vision for the future. Entitlement is big in this generation. Learning more of their rights, rather than their responsibilities, a philosophy of entitlement has emerged that says, "I deserve to have this, or they owe me this and so on …" This philosophy has robbed our kids of their visions and dreams. Walking in a world without challenges or deadlines has weakened this generation's resolve to fight and stand for the truth.

- PHYSICALLY MATURING EARLIER.

  Even just taking a simple look at the fashion of young people today, it is obvious that they seem to mature earlier in life. They are conscious of physical senses and drives early in their development. The sixteen year olds of yesterday are the 13'ers of today. Of course, it depends on where a person lives, rural or urban. But when I refer to teenagers, I refer to the average young teens today. In a whole spectrum of teenagers today, I refer to the average, where generally they are exposed to TV, movies and computers. Exposure accelerated their physical maturity or awareness of the social or moral issues.

- MAJOR DECISIONS SOONER.

  Facing mature demands in life early forces the young generation to make major decisions earlier than expected. For example, teenage mothers decide the future of their children early in life, even before they are prepared for motherhood.

- LOSS OF FAMILY STRUCTURE.

  This phenomenon is on the rise over the last 50 years. The family structure is being attacked in every continent of the world. The one child policy of China, the decreasing birth rate in Europe, the rate of abortion in America, and child trafficking in Asia are mere symptoms of the breakdown of this structure. We have a whole generation in China today that has no cousins, uncles and aunts. The death rate is higher than the birth rate in Europe. This seems to be a sign of a dying culture. And the estimated total abortion of babies for the last 40 years is over one billion children. That is simply shocking. These social issues all contribute to weakening the family structure. This breakdown takes away a powerful support for the young generation to cope with the pressure of the Media culture.

- UNSUPERVISED FREE TIME.

    Young people of today do not usually have adult supervision when they spend their free time. Many times during these free times, choices in life are made in the absence of adult predetermined boundaries. Because of this I have always said that the new idol of young people today is their precious free time. They will rarely give it up for anything, unless they really like the alternative. If you can get a young person to surrender his or her free time, you get a strong commitment.

- NO MORAL ANCHOR IN SOCIETY.

    The culture of young people today is getting confused due to globalization. Morality becomes subjective, and complicated issues on values are presented usually without a ready answer. Moral issues are now cultural issues and the absolutes are slowly disintegrating. Any RIGHT can be made WRONG and vice versa, leaving a generation that doesn't have an anchor to hold on to, before it goes over the cliff of chaos or immoral abyss.

- INABILITY TO COPE.

    This seems to be a much stressed-out generation. Because of that, suicide is on a steady rise among the young, even though we have been described as a Youth-Obsessed Culture, because everything is about the youth: products are designed for them, computer items are designed to be youth friendly, advertising aims to lure the youth ... Yet, it only makes a generation more and more isolated. Social Media is diminishing the social skills of the young. Isolation is the precursor to self-destruction because we are all created to be social beings.

Because of these, the Digital Culture exhibits destructive reactions. Here are some of them.

- NUMBING EFFECT

    When young people reach teenage life, just by watching TV or movies regularly, most of them would have witnessed thousands of TV murders, a lot of infidelity, family breakdowns and most of the cultural ills a society can offer. They become insensitive. One person once said, "When you've lived in the sewer for so long, you don't know how bad it smells." As one is desensitized to the smell due to overexposure, so is the young generation insensitive to the moral and social ills due to overexposure in the media.

- ABANDONMENT SYNDROME

    When young people today cannot find meaning in what

they are doing, most of them will say the same word, "I'm bored." Continuous boredom will drive them to look for things they can claim as their significance. When they find it, they live in abandon to it. It may be sports, music, drugs or even alcohol.

- PARTY TILL YOU DROP PHILOSOPHY

    We have a generation that potentially doesn't have to sleep. Because of the 24/7 available media, a hedonistic philosophy is rising. Spend yourself in entertainment until you are exhausted. Night is turned into day when it comes to diversions. Unlimited entertainment, implying that your stamina for it is the only limitation, because it's a buffet of entertainment—"enjoy all you can"—life. What a perverted philosophy! If you can take it, you can enjoy it.

- WITHDRAW OR ISOLATION

    Computer games are becoming more and more sophisticated and complicated. Phone Game Apps meanwhile are created to deal with boredom of young people. It keeps them busy while waiting for a bus, lining up for school work … etc. So the digital culture is starting to minimize face-to-face interaction. Unintentional withdrawal ends up as unwanted isolation. This contributes to the "Party Till You Drop" philosophy.

- UNPLUGGED

    Teenage suicide today is estimated at 1 million per year

globally. It is one of the three leading causes of death among teenagers. It outnumbers deaths due to armed conflicts. The Digital culture can swing into extreme isolation which eventually can cause many mental issues. If they don't find their destiny, they will self-destruct.[2]

---

2. www.moh.org/ leadership materials by Winkie Pratney, entitled *Digital Generation: Ministry at the Millennium.*

Chapter 7

THE GREATEST NEEDS
OF THIS GENERATION

As I continued to minister to the emerging generation of digitals, I noted three distinct needs unite them all. Once these needs are met, digitals will be loyal and committed to you or your group. Any brotherhood or fraternity can impersonate to meet these needs.

- DESTINY

    Digitals are looking for purpose. If they are disconnected to the older generation, they will seek connection elsewhere. When I was in the Netherlands, I ministered to a group of young adults. As I ended with an altar call to pray for their nation, one 17-year-old, young lady came weeping and praying for Holland. After crying for some time, she stood up and thanked me for giving her destiny. I was speechless.

    "For if you are completely silent at this time, relief and deliverance shall arise to the Jews from another place, but you and your father's house shall be destroyed. And who knows whether you have come to the kingdom for a time like this?" (Esther 4:14)

- MILITANCY

  We have a very under-challenged Generation of Digitals. Old Timers like me could underestimate their capacity to learn, innovate and lead. We teach them our old methods and structures when they have better alternatives in their generation. Because of giving them tasks that are way beneath their capacity, we turn their passion into mediocrity. We actually suppress them. Those who capitalize on this are the extremists, and they sometimes get the best of our youth because they actually have more to offer than the programs in our churches. We actually lose by default as we have a very weak offer to a very powerful generation.

  "Your people will freely join you, resplendent in holy armor on the great day of your conquest. Join you at the fresh break of day, join you with all the vigor of youth" (Psalm 110:3).

- FAMILY

  The greatest unspoken need of digitals is a sense of family. As family structures continue to disintegrate, more and more young people will look for social alternatives. Brotherhoods, gangs and many common interest groups will inadequately be used as a substitute to family. If the Church doesn't adopt these digitals as family, many counterfeits will arise.

"And let the peace of God rule in your hearts, to which you also are called in one body, and be thankful" (Colossians 3:15).

The spirit and power of Elijah expressed in Fathering can meet these needs of a young person in the digital age. The Church that emphasizes its role as the family of God will gain their loyalty. When they are treated as sons and daughters and not merely a statistic in a report, they will emerge at their best. And they are a powerful generation!

Chapter 8

TURNING MEDIOCRITY INTO A 'NO COMPROMISE' LIFESTYLE

Are we headed for another but more powerful Jesus Movement?

How do you minister to a Digital Generation? How can this Millennial Generation rediscover their destiny?

It will take more than just adapting their tools and gadgets and lifestyle or fashion. I once met a pastor who literally started wearing hip hop clothes, earrings and tattoos in order to connect or identify with the young generation. But when you see a 50-year-old man, wearing oversized, low waist-baggy pants, you smell something is fake. And that is what turns off the young people.

When people are not real, 'A Hypersensitivity to Hypocrisy' has developed. The reason why "Reality TV shows" get the highest rating on TV shows is because we have a generation crying out for reality.

They have seen the best actors and actresses in Hollywood; they voted them to win by buying the tickets and following them. They have watched the unbelievably realistic special effects of "Lord of the Rings" and what's on PlayStation and Xbox. They are keen to know what is real and what is not. So when they come to church, they can detect if the Pastor is just doing some special effects on stage or if God is really there. We are ministering to experts on special effects, so let us beware not to appear as amateur imitators to them. They will know if an encounter with God is real or fake. And God wants them to encounter Him.

Let me share with you a summary chart written by Winkie Pratney. (Digital Generation: Ministry at the Millennium edge published on the Ministry of Helps website, www.moh.org/ 1999, Winkie Pratney. Contact at Box 876, Lindale, TX. 75771.) See how real these characteristics are and how our responses have to change to meet the needs of this young generation. If we need to make an impact in this generation, we have to change.

CHARACTERISTICS	CORRESPONDING RESPONSE
1. Highly Visual Sensitive to Hypocrisy, Hungry for reality	**• Deeply Real** Transparency, Genuine Affection
2. Casually Technological Comfortable with Digital Tools	**• Genuinely Personal** Committed to Practical Discipleship
3. Shamed No Guilt or True God, Blamed for Everything	**• Embraced** Honored as Humanity, Forgiven for Failure
4. Scattered Orphaned, Abandoned and Alone	**• Adopted** Treated as Family, Mobilized as an Army
5. Scorned Treated as Lepers, Feared as Destroyers	**• Accepted** Welcomed as Believers, Trusted as Builders
6. Rejected Perceived as Misfits, Discarded as Useless	**• Elected** Prophesied as Missionaries, Valued Worthy
7. Discouraged Overwhelmed by Stress and Pressure	**• Encouraged** Called to Bravery, Ministered to for Ministry
8. Extreme Lifestyle No Reservation for Self-Preservation	**• Digital Message** No Compromise Call to Holiness and Truth

Once we turn this into our daily guide to minister to digitals, we will be able to touch them and release them to their destiny. It seems simple and straightforward, but it would mean hard work and one-on-one ministry. We can't treat them like an element in a production line, throw a young person into a process and then out comes a disciple of Jesus. That is exactly what will repel them. How difficult is this?

Chapter 9

VAMPIRES AND ZOMBIES CULTURE—WHAT'S THE FUZZ ABOUT?

Why is this generation obsessed with Vampires and Zombies? The increasing number of movies with these themes is significantly noticeable because it seems if any movie will have just either of these two elements, it will be a hit ... meaning, the youth will patronize it. Why?

Movie trends are a reflection of the culture's real, hidden need or desire. Does the resurgence of movies with comic heroes show a desire for a Savior? Can very well be ... or when movies with hidden supernatural powers are released and harnessed for good, do they show a hunger for significance in a big world? Could very well be. But what about Zombies and Vampires?

The logical inference I could get is that it reveals a desire for everlasting life, when one can live forever and love forever. We have a generation who is hungry for a Savior, supernatural powers and everlasting life. If so, the Church would be most relevant today because that is what God gives to every believer, isn't it?

What a setup it seems to be. It is a preparation for Elijah, the superhero of the Old Testament, has to come. Even the culture says the fullness of time has come.

PART 2

THE SYNERGY

THE SPIRIT AND POWER OF AN ANCIENT NAZARITE Connecting the ANCIENT PATH to the PRESENT GENERATION.

Generational Transfer—a fusion between two generations, one OLDER and the other CURRENT.

In Malachi 4: 5-6, God promised to send an Ancient Hero into our present world, current generation to bring back an ancient path of fathering that would have been forgotten.

A TERMINATOR from the PAST is sent to teach us a lesson today?

> "Behold, I am going to send you Elijah the prophet before the coming of the great and terrible day of the Lord. He will restore the hearts of the fathers to their children and the hearts of the children to their fathers, so that I will not come and smite the land with a curse" (Malachi 4:5-6).

The message translation makes it even clearer:

> "But also look ahead: I'm sending Elijah the prophet to clear the way for the Big Day of God—the decisive Judgment Day."

Now this sounds like a Terminator is being sent to us for Judgment Day. Even the language sounds like current generation language.

What is the spirit and power of Elijah? What is he going to accomplish by turning the hearts of the Fathers to the sons? That sounds easy enough. Why ask an Ancient Man from the past to do it? What is his specialty? Father and son heart-turner?

Of course, there is more to it than it looks. One needs to understand who Elijah is and what he represents. What is the issue of generations today between fathers and sons? Why is there a gap? Why is there a disconnect? Is it that serious that God needed to send someone from the Ancients to come and mend the gap?

Chapter 10

ISOLATION KILLS
GOD'S MOVE AND VISION

It is the strategy to deter this
generation from achieving its destiny.

A respected Professor, Philip Zimbardo, an authority on psychology from Stanford University states:

"I know of no more potent killer than isolation. There is no more destructive influence on physical and mental health than the isolation of you from me and us from them. It has been shown to be a central agent in the etiology of depression, paranoia, schizophrenia, rape, suicide, mass murder, and a wide variety of disease states."

And, he goes on to add:

"The devil's strategy for our times is to trivialize human existence and to isolate us from one another while creating the delusion that the reasons are time pressures, work demands, or economic strategies."

In Dennis Rainey's book *Staying Close*: stopping the natural drift towards isolation in marriage, page 5, it states that there is no more potent killer than **isolation**. Isolation destroys your mind and your emotions. The report says it is the cause of depression, all kinds of mental illness, and even mass murder and suicide. If you isolate a person, a person goes crazy.

God intended for the link between the generations to never be broken. He fondly identifies Himself as the God of Abraham, Isaac and Jacob. God wasn't name-dropping famous people, He was illustrating that His purposes and vision goes on from one generation to the next. A seamless movement from one generation to the next is necessary for His vision to be fulfilled. God's vision outlives a generation, so it is necessary that it be transferred to the next generation clearly and smoothly. Only when there is no gap can this be done as God designed it to be.

Unfortunately today, we are seeing not just a generation gap, but a canyon wide separation between the Millennial Generation and the previous generations. The many reasons are stated earlier in this book, the unique and fast thinking, fast talking generation we have has isolated itself. Perceived to be different, young people know that to pursue understanding with the older generation is frustrating.

Chapter 11

RESTORING THE LINK
BETWEEN THE GENERATIONS

Elijah's main task is sent to **RESTORE** this link.

A hero from the past is sent to rescue the present generation and save the world. This sounds like a storyline from a Marvel movie. But it is what needs to happen. An Isolated Generation will kill God's vision and plan. Satan makes every effort to destroy this generation or distract it. The best way is keep it isolated. And the technological advances we have today are keeping young people glued to their gadgets, rather than a face-to-face interaction with people, not to mention an older generation who still couldn't get used to Skype calls and chatrooms.

Studies show that if you isolate a person, a person inevitably loses sanity and either kills himself or kills others. If you isolate a nation, a nation will die. Because of our global economy, an isolated economy would not survive. It will collapse. If you isolate a church, a church will eventually suffocate, because it was designed for community and a community of churches is necessary to touch nations.

Paul wrote to the churches in cities, building a link between the churches … but when you isolate a generation, the vision of God dies—His move dies and His purposes are buried with the previous generation.

In Judges it says,

"Eventually that entire generation died and was buried. Then another generation grew up that didn't know anything of God or the work he had done for Israel" (Judges 2:10).

This is an example that the generational link was broken and how does one restore it? A Hero like an Elijah has to come … to restore it.

Now if you apply that today, we need Elijah more than any other generation. Because the gap today is not only wide, but continuously growing. The reason is this generation is isolating more and more. Unless the older generation will get a fresh desire and passion for the younger ones, not just their biological children, but the generation previous, the gap will continue to grow.

Also, unless the digital generation will be willing to humble themselves and get a fresh love and respect for the older generation, they will remain in their isolated state.

Chapter 12

THE POWER TO BREAK THE ISOLATION AND RESTORE THE LINK

For this reason, we need the spirit and power of Elijah. God is not sending a Hero from the past to conduct a mere emotional reconciliation between a father and a son, but to do a very complicated process of mending the generational link by touching the old and at the same time the young. It has to be a two-way move. That is why it is not just a youth movement, but a two generations movement. Without both, isolation will win.

When I got saved in the Jesus Movement, we experienced a youth revival like no other. So many were getting saved, turning to God … the beaches of Los Angeles, California, were venues for massive baptisms because so many were turning to God. This movement was not led by one specific group or person, but was led by the Holy Spirit. However, after a few years, the movement died.

The older generation of believers rejected the form of the Jesus Movement because this young generation was extreme, long haired, ragged and very informal. Many of them saved from the hippies of the 60's. Church doors were closed and many new believers fell away.

After a few years, the movement died. Why? Isolation. Satan shot it dead by keeping the two generations apart. This is evident in the prejudices between the generations. We had a saying going around in those days, "You can't trust anybody who is above 30 years old."

Ironically, at the same time, The Women's Liberation movement was born, the Civil Rights movement started and even the Gay Rights movement began. And all those movements are still here, but the Jesus Movement is dead. Why? Because it was a movement propelled only by the youth—one generation. It did not include the older generation. Satan knows that if he can break the link, he could kill the move of God. And so he did.

If we are going to have another Jesus Movement all over the world, we must make sure that the link is never broken between the two generations. This is why the spirit and power of Elijah is necessary to secure the link and keep the passion and fire for each generation burning.

A battle cry that summarizes it all is: Where are the fathers and mothers who will live for the destiny of their spiritual children? Where are the sons and daughters who would live for the honor of their spiritual parents?

This is a GENERATIONAL TRANSFER, when one generation secures the flow of God's vision and moves to the next generation. This makes the present generation more powerful. As all the strength of the previous generation rests in them … the God of Abraham, Isaac and Jacob.

God had foreseen this thousands of years ago that there would be a generation that is so powerful and unique that they will be hard to understand or even accept, so He prophesied that He would have to send Elijah, the prophet, to break the isolation and restore the link between the generations in order to fulfill God's end time plan. So here we are today, struggling with our teenagers at home and in church.

I have seen this synergy between the generations lost in many nations. Revival broke out somewhere, but that revival is never transferred. The result is that the place where revival took place ends up in worse condition than it was before the revival. Even Wales, a country that experienced the most powerful revival the world has ever seen, is today struggling with church growth. Why? Have we lost the art of Generational Transfer? Have we forgotten how the Ancients have done it?

It is interesting that in Malachi 4:6, it says that once the link was restored, the curse on the land is removed. That is a promise of power. The curse will be lifted, defeated or cancelled once the link between fathers and sons are restored.

Our spiritual land is cursed, I see. Before, when you shared the Gospel many responded, today … people are not responding as before. I used to say that when there is revival, EVERYTHING works. Every strategy, no matter how silly, they all work. People respond and are getting saved. We would play guitars on the street corners in front of schools and we'd get a crowd and people responded. Today, almost nothing works. A total opposite. Even the best strategy you can find, it seems to bring in a very little harvest, or as the fishermen would say,

"The fish ain't biting!" Is it possible that the spiritual land is cursed?

When do you say a land is cursed? If you plant a sack of wheat, you expect to harvest maybe 50 sacks after the planting season. Then, you will say that the land is good. But if you plant a sack and you harvest half a sack, you will say that land is cursed. Not a good land.

Today, many pastors are burning out. Why? It's because many are overworked; yet, it yields very little fruit or harvest. Is it possible that the land is cursed and we need the spirit and power of Elijah to restore the link and remove the curses in our cities and our nations?

This is the reason we need to go back to the Ancient Path. The Path of Elijah, where the link is never broken and the curse is always lifted. And revival can come anytime.

In Jeremiah 6:16, it says,

"Thus says the Lord, 'Stand by the ways and see and ask for the ancient paths, Where the good way is, and walk in it; and you will find rest for your souls.'"

Let us rediscover the Ancient Path, and find rest for a burnt out lifestyle.

What is this ancient path?

Elijah gives us a clue and an understanding. He was perceived to be a Nazarite. Therefore, the path of a Nazarite seems to be God's ancient path.

PART 3

THE ANCIENT PATH
REDISCOVERED

When you hear the term Nazarite you wonder what that really means. If it isn't a new slimming diet or an old martial arts revival, what then is it? Others, who are more history sensitive, say that it can mean the revival of a World War II ritual of recruitment—Nazi Rite. All these, of course, have no connection to the biblical concept of a Nazarite.

In order to capture the significance of this book, let us examine the Nazarite concept in the Bible, and then discover its present-day relevance.

Nazarites are Old Testament National leaders who took the meaning of commitment to the highest level. They became God's grace to the spiraling moral degradation of Israel during that time. When necessary, they even became the deliverers of Israel—Samson, Samuel, and Elijah. They voluntarily make an explicit vow as stated in Numbers 6:2-8,

(2) Speak to the sons of Israel, and say to them, when a man or a woman shall vow a vow, a vow of a Nazirite, to be separated to Jehovah,

(3) He shall separate from wine and strong drink and shall drink no vinegar of wine, or vinegar of strong drink; neither shall he drink any liquor of grapes, nor eat moist grapes or dried.

(4) All the days of his Nazariteship he shall eat nothing that is made of the grapevine, from grape seeds even to a stem.

(5) All the days of his vow to separate, no razor shall come upon his head. Until all the days are fulfilled in which he separates to Jehovah, he shall be holy. He

shall let the locks of the hair of his head grow.

(6) All the days that he separates to Jehovah, he shall not come near any dead body.

(7) He shall not make himself unclean for his father, or for his mother, or for his brother, or for his sister, when they die, because his separation to his God is upon his head.

(8) All the days of his separation he is holy to Jehovah.

These vows may seem extreme, even to those who lived in Israel at that time. They were meant to be. Although voluntary, the significance of the terms of their vow can speak to all of us. Their commitment honors God and shows us in a minute way His desire to see total dedication from His people.

Chapter 13

THE PATH AND CODE
OF THE NAZARITE

Their vow can be categorized into three: Not to drink wine; not to cut his/her hair; not to come near a dead body.

Obviously, to simply exercise these restraints does not necessarily make one a genuine Nazarite, for religions all over the world throughout the ages have produced dedication more extreme than these. Men have practiced total seclusion from society and its pleasures, while others, not being contented with it, went further by self-inflicting physical pain and suffering. These religious standards make the Nazarite vow child's play.

There is definitely more to it than not visiting the salon for the rest of one's adult life or missing all the funerals of your entire family. It is also not just another version of the South Beach diet.

The key to the Nazarite vow is the phrase *"separated to Jehovah (holy)."* Without this phrase it simply becomes a self-imposed discipline that doesn't have any physical, social or even spiritual benefit.

To be separated for God through these three categories or terms has deeper significance. Let me bring out on the following page what I think it speaks about.

The 3 H Code of a Nazarite includes:

- Humility
- Hunger
- Holiness

We will look at these three areas in the next few chapters.

Chapter 14

THE CODE OF HUMILITY

To not drink wine would require Humility.
(An inner strength to stand against social pressure).

The Ancient Path of HUMILITY: A Nazarite makes a vow of Humility. He/she expresses this by giving up his/her legitimate rights (typified by not drinking any wine). We all know that humility is a character trait or a virtue. How does one move from a vow to a lifestyle? How do we produce the virtue of Humility in our lives?

Humility is difficult to define. It can be seen as an act, a habit or a lifestyle. Some people think that it is temperament based. When a person is more introverted then he looks humble. On the other hand, when someone is outgoing or extroverted, they have a greater tendency to be prideful. If these were true, then to change our character would mean to change our temperaments. I disagree. It is true that we are all new in Christ, according to 2 Corinthians 5:17. But this doesn't necessarily mean that God gives us a "personality transplant."

Although Moses learned meekness after 40 years in the wilderness, while shepherding, learning to put rage under control, he still has the same basic personality when he left

Egypt the first time. He still is as passionate for his people, the Hebrews, as before. When he first left Egypt, he was running away from a crime of passion because he killed one man. The second time he left Egypt was to lead around two million people to the Promise Land. To lead two million people would definitely require real passion, too. What was different was not his personality. His passion for his people remained, but his maturity had grown.

To learn humility doesn't mean God will change our basic temperaments. God's plan is not to make us all look alike in personalities. It is not like in the movies when Aliens take over the human race and everyone walk and talk the same way. God doesn't wipe out our personalities, but He matures them through a process called transformation.

So what then is humility? Why does God put a lot of importance to learning humility? Micah 6:8 says that God requires three things of us: do justly, love kindness and to walk HUMBLY with our God. Humility is a walk with God, a journey. This journey has a beginning and an end. Every step with God brings us closer to the goal of transformation. The Bible says we go from glory to glory in this walk.

Humility is a "mother trait." This means from it will come other character traits. Humility is the parent of Integrity, Loyalty, Honor, Patience, Endurance, Meekness, Self-Control, Godliness … and many others. It is like a fountainhead, from where all the other traits flow. If one practices Humility, other character traits will develop.

However, let me describe Humility as a path one takes, and every path or journey begins with steps. The first step in this journey is 'Knowing Who We Are' and being willing to accept that. This would mean that we are willing to face ourselves and understand the reason for our attitudes. In this section, we understand humility by defining pride.

Understanding pride reveals things in our lives that feed it. Pride (thinking of ourselves higher or lower than who we really are) is encouraged by our wrong self-perception. This makes our world smaller as we become limited by what we think we are. God wants to break you out of this prison and free you to be who He called you to be. Pride shrinks our world, and to be humble opens it up to many new possibilities.

Let us walk this journey together.

> "O people, the Lord has told you what is good, and this is what he requires of you: to do what is right, to love mercy and to walk humbly with your God" (Micah 6:8).

> "God opposes the proud but favors the humble" (James 4:6).

> "Humble yourselves before the Lord, and he will lift you up in honor" (James 4:10).

> "The fear of the Lord teaches wisdom; humility precedes honor" (Proverbs 15:33).

"True humility and fear of the Lord lead to riches, honor and long life" (Proverbs 22:4).

If my people who are called by my name will humbles themselves ..." (2 Chronicles 7:14).

This is perhaps the hardest of the Nazarite Code. Our Hunger for God starts with being Humble, and we can only maintain a Holy walk if we keep walking in Humility. This may be the hardest of all the Nazarite vows, but it is also the most powerful.

Chapter 15

THE CODE OF HUNGER FOR GOD

To not cut one's hair is a symbol of Intimacy.
(A growing reminder of one's time spent with God).

Previously, we talked about Humility, our nature and who we really are, the key to walking in Humility. Now we will talk about turning our Hunger/Thirst for God into a lifestyle of chasing after the things of God. A Nazarite's code of Hunger for God is displayed in the length of their hair. It is the only visible display of this Nazarite vow. The longer one's hair is reflects on how long he or she has committed to the vow. Samson, a Nazarite since birth, would have pretty long hair. Why would someone do this for a prolonged period of time? The only reason is because he is after God in his life. That is why if you lose your hair, it symbolizes that you have lost your hunger for God.

However, before we discuss lifestyle change, we should ask the first question. Are we really hungry for Him? Are we really thirsty for His life and His living water? Is our hunger and thirst for Him genuine?

This is the first question we should ask ... then we could move on to a lifestyle change. It is like taking a course in college. Before we talk about how to be an engineer or a doctor, the first question we need to settle is do we really want to be an engineer or do we want to be a doctor? Is our desire to pursue this course genuine? If not, then we will be wasting our time in studying. It is the same here.

Before we learn to 'cultivate' our hunger for God, we need to make sure that we are *truly* hungry for Him and not merely *mistake* our appetites, our physical drives for our *deep* spiritual cry for Divine satisfaction.

How REAL is our hunger? This will determine whether or not we will last in the path of Hunger for God. We need to find out for ourselves if we are hungry for God or just for His blessings. Are we using God for our own health, wealth and prosperity cravings and not really for the inner yearnings of our soul and spirit?

When Jesus spoke to the Samaritan woman in John, chapter 4, He intentionally stirred up her thirst for "living water." All the while this thirst was in her, but she wasn't aware of it. She was trying to satisfy this thirst through relationships (having five husbands). It is easy to replace our appetite for God with other physical appetites, which causes us to chase after the proverbial end of the rainbow.

The pure Hunger or Thirst for God will be detected by Heaven, and God will respond to it.

Chapter 16

THE CODE OF HOLINESS

And to not touch any dead body obviously represents Purity.
(A symbol of a person's determination
to be free from contamination).

Holiness is unique to God, so we have a hard time understating the concept that God is holy. We first must realize that this characteristic is exclusive to God. In my own words, whenever we say God is holy it would mean this:

"THAT GOD IS UNIQUELY, ABSOLUTELY, DISTINCTIVELY PERFECT IN EVERY THING, EXCLUSIVE AND COMPLETE IN SUBSTANCE AND SUPREME AND MATCHLESS IN VALUE, UTMOST IN WORTH AND SIGNIFICANCE AND IRREPLACEABLE IN ALL PAST, PRESENT AND FUTURE CREATED BEINGS."

This absolute value and worth is only accorded to God. This distinct perfection is characteristic of only one Being, God! This exclusive and all-encompassing substance can only be found in God! This highest worth and significance will only be seen in the only Uncreated Being, God! Recognizing God's 'value' obligates us to choose Him or what is His Highest good as the wisest possible act. A Choice for God is a choice for all our good. We call this the Law of love. To be holy is to choose to obey this Love Law.

A Nazarite makes a vow of Holiness. This lifestyle is different from the legalistic lifestyle of the religious leaders of Jesus' time. It is not based on rules and rituals, but on God's Law of Love. Choosing God's highest good as the wisest possible act of a moral being restores a Godly system of values on earth. It, therefore, can spark reformation in nations.

This law of being valuable, based on God's nature and character, becomes the foundation of a lifestyle of Loving God—producing Holiness. A revival of Holiness is actually an awakening of the moral conscience of society. When people live a lifestyle of Holiness, based on loving God, the moral conscience is awakened and somehow can reverse the downward spiraling of morality in our land.

In simple terms, true Reformation starts with resetting the moral conscience of society. Our consciences have a factory setting, just like when you buy a mobile phone. Resetting our moral consciences will bring social reformation.

These three inner strengths or qualities are constantly developed through the Nazarite vow. One exercises humility, intimacy and purity, day after day throughout the duration of the vow. These same qualities are rare today as we have a generation pressured to be famous, achieve social status and a 'make a name for himself' philosophy.

Global communications and media have amplified these pressures. Just as one's success can be congratulated by the whole world so is one's failure condemned the same way. So now we watch as the world witnesses the success of the proud, boastful and arrogant atheist, and then shocked, humiliated and scandalized by a religious leader in grave contrast.

Can the Nazarite vow be an expression of God's desire for an emerging generation?

In the Old Testament, we learn from Numbers, chapter 6, that anyone who desires to be a Nazarite essentially makes three vows. These vows are a day-to-day act that through time turns into a lifestyle. It is true we don't have literal Nazarites today because we are under a new covenant through Jesus Christ. Jesus was not a Nazarite; neither were any of the apostles. Although they did not practice the vows, they lived the lifestyle an Old Testament Nazarite would be expected to live.

Chapter 17

THE NAZARITE VOWS IN THE NEW TESTAMENT

Jesus was tempted in the wilderness three times before He began his ministry. (Matthew, chapter 4 and Luke, chapter 4). It is significant to note that each temptation targeted a specific weakness in mankind that throughout history has proven to be the most vulnerable areas.

In an overview we see the three major temptations—the three strongest internal enemies of mankind in 1 John 2:16:

- "Command this stone that it become bread" appeals to the lust of the flesh, especially if you have not eaten for 40 days.
- When Satan showed Jesus the glory of all the kingdoms, it awakened the lust of the eyes.
- To throw Himself from the pinnacle of the temple and have angels miraculously save Him just to prove His authority awakens the Pride of life.

Although Jesus answered every temptation with Scripture, it is obvious that these were not merely memory checks; they were tests of consecration. Was Jesus living a consecrated lifestyle? Yes, He was, and in three major areas, thus three areas of testing.

THE LUST OF THE FLESH WAS A TEST OF HIS HUNGER FOR GOD.

Many times we fail in our mere appetites, not only for food, but also our hunger for entertainment, achievement, material things, money, etc. These things are amoral, neither right nor wrong, just as "turning stone into bread." What makes them wrong is when we replace them for our hunger for God.

Christians have too many distractions today. Our calendars are cluttered with activities. The activities themselves are not wrong, but when the nonessentials take over, we lose our real desire for God. The lust of the flesh takes over and turns every stone, not just into bread, but also into every desirable thing.

THE LUST OF THE EYES WAS A TEST OF HIS HOLINESS.

The eye is the gate to almost everything. "Your eye is a lamp that provides light for your body. When your eye is good, your whole body is filled with light … if you are filled with light, with no dark corners, then your whole life will be radiant, as though a floodlight were filling you with light." (Luke 11:34-36). To keep oneself pure starts with our thoughts, which is basically stimulated with our eyes or our senses.

What a temptation it would be to see the glory of all the kingdoms and then have them offered to you on a silver plate! How can that be wrong? Can't we use it for the glory of God? No, we can't. Because if we receive it from a source other than God, we are replacing Him as the object of our worship. This is why the condition to receive these kingdoms is to bow down to the tempter, meaning replace God in your life.

From whom did we receive what we have? Who do we owe our good life to? There are only two sources of material blessings: God and the world (of course, this includes the tempter). To choose God is the highest choice. It brings holiness.

THE PRIDE OF LIFE WAS A TEST OF HIS HUMILITY.

Angels would have saved Jesus if He fell off the pinnacle of the temple. But to do it in the way it was presented by the tempter in the wilderness would have put God to the test. Not a test of ability, for surely God can catch anyone who is falling. However, it would have tested God's authority—provoking God to respond just to validate a person's sense of control. Jesus' answer declared that only God has ultimate authority, and He is not accountable to us. God is not accountable to anyone. He is God, and we are not.

Jesus Revolution Now started a Nazarite Training years ago to bring Millennials to the Ancient Path of the Nazarite. This training is not aimed at producing longhaired freaks who don't attend funerals and never drink an alcoholic beverage, but gulps all the Starbucks coffee they can get. No, it isn't meant for that. The goal is to release a generation, living a consecrated lifestyle not characterized by a religiosity expressed in legalism, but a spirituality, conveyed through humility, hunger and a holiness for God.

Today, God seems to be pouring out His grace once more over our societies. The borderless youth culture of today is asking more from Christianity than ever before. They are under challenged, digital (technologically advanced), and under great attack. The present generation is restless and hungry for a cause that will match their unique DNA. Could this be the generation God has been waiting for? Is God raising up a whole generation of Nazarites as one of his expressions of grace?

In Amos 2:12, God counted it as sin when Israel "(made) the Nazarites drink wine." Maybe we, as a church hinder God by causing this generation to live in mediocrity and discourage them to make a commitment of the highest level. In essence, we may have asked the present day Nazarites to drink present day wine, so to speak.

This is the main reason why Jesus Revolution Now is starting the Nazarite Training. The goal is to build a strong foundation of character in order to build anointings and giftings. Therefore, release this generation to one of the greatest challenges the Church has ever faced, to turn nations back to God.

It is time to call this generation to fulfill the Nazarite vow: a commitment to Humility, Purity and Intimacy.

Chapter 18

THE IMPACT OF A
NAZARITE LIFESTYLE

These same qualities are repeated by God in the mostly quoted passage to bring healing to the nations found in 2 Chronicles 7:14,

> *"If My People who are called by my name will*
> *Humble themselves, Pray and Seek my Face and*
> *Turn from their wicked ways ... then I will hear ...*
> *forgive ... and heal their land."*

This passage gives us a formula:

Humility + Hunger + Holiness =
God will hear + God will forgive + God will heal our land.

Amazingly these requirements are the same qualities emphasized by the Nazarite vow.

TRANSFORMATION EQUATION

HUMILITY

HUNGER

HOLINESS

TRANSFORMATION

I will hear
I will forgive
I will heal

I used to ask the question, "Can God speak to a whole Church?" Oh, yes, He can.

"Can God speak to a whole nation? Just one message to a whole country?" Yes, He can.

"But can God speak to a whole generation?" Yes, He can! So I will share with you what I believe God's message is to a whole generation.

John the Baptist had only one message, "Repent for the Kingdom of God is at hand." And it lasted him a whole lifetime of preaching the same message. I believe God has one message for this generation. It is a message of getting back to the consecration you once had, the sacrifice you once were willing to make, the commitment you as a person and as a Church once had. These are all summarized in the Nazarite Lifestyle of Humility, Hunger and Holiness for God. God can remove the curse of our land and bring healing if we practice it.

2 Chronicles 7:14 is usually a theme in prayer movement events. "Let's do a 2 Chronicles 7:14" ... but I have sometimes spoken up and said, "We can't do a 2 Chronicles 7:14; we have to "BE" 2 Chronicles 7:14."

If we live in Humility, and Hunger for God and pursue Holiness, then God will come and heal our land. This, I think, is the John the Baptist message for our generation.

Chapter 19

DEVELOPING A NAZARITE GENERATION

"The earth belongs to the Lord. Everything in it belongs to Him ... This is the generation of those who seek Him, who seek Your face. Oh God of Jacob" (Psalm 24:1-6).

Now, everybody in the world believes that there is a coming powerful generation. All international leaders, from Loren Cunningham to Bill Bright, believe that there is a coming, powerful generation. They all believe that this generation will have one simple task. This generation will turn nations back to God with a great harvest of souls. This coming generation will be so powerful that it will transform nations.

Psalm 24:6 says that this is the generation who will seek Him. I don't know if you accept this. Because I believe God has a purpose for every generation. You can probably see it in the history of your country.

Let's look at the history of my nation, the Philippines. We were under Spain for almost 400 years. During those years we almost never resisted the Spaniards. The Spaniards suppressed us and did all kinds of oppressive things, but we never resisted them. After 400 years, in one generation, in one time, the whole generation rose up against the Spaniards and won our freedom. It was like a generation of heroes was born. It was like the purpose of that generation alone was to get us freedom.

Now, if you examine the history of your nation, you would see certain times in your country where a generation is born for a specific purpose. This is what I believe we are seeing today. I believe we are about to see a generation rise up who will be more powerful than any other generation in the history of the Church. The Bible prophesies it! All the great men and women of God are waiting for it.

Can there be a whole generation whose sole DNA is to seek after God? We are seeing a powerful prayer movement spreading all over the world. We are seeing young people who are really determined to serve God—to fast and pray for the nation. We're starting to see a different kind of generation rising up. I believe it's a generation of forerunners or worship warriors.

In Psalm 110:3, it says,

"On the day you fight your enemies your young
people will volunteer. Like the dew of early the
morning, your young men will come to you on
the sacred hills."

In this verse it says that your young people will be like the dew of the morning. It implies that there will be a massive number of young volunteers you cannot stop from coming to church. It is a prophetic verse that speaks of a generation where thousands and thousands of young people will be fighting for our nation.

It also says in Luke 1:17, when the prophecy about John the Baptist came, and it says there,

"John the Baptist will go before Him in the spirit and power of Elijah to turn the hearts of the fathers to the children and the disobedient to the wisdom of the just, to make a ready a people prepared for the Lord."

Come on brothers and sisters, you need to catch this.

In the ministry of John the Baptist, he never performed a single miracle. John the Baptist is not a signs and wonders prophet. He didn't raise the dead, he didn't heal the sick. Yet, Jesus said that he was the most powerful prophet who ever lived. Why? You know what John the Baptist did? He resurrected a dead generation! His message was for a whole generation. And the same spirit and power of Elijah is coming today.

We go to Malachi 4:5, 6. Here it says,

"I am sending you Elijah the before the great and dreadful day of Jehovah. And he shall turn the hearts of the fathers to the sons, and the hearts of the sons to the fathers. That I not come and strike the earth with utter destruction."

You know when I read this verse, I asked the Lord a question. Because when the great and dreadful day comes, we need a powerful prophet. And God says He'll send the spirit and power of Elijah, and Elijah is the most powerful prophet in the Old Testament. Because Elijah can call fire from Heaven anytime he wants. Have you seen anyone do that today? Call fire from Heaven? Very powerful prophet! Elijah has authority over the weather. So, God sends Elijah, the most powerful prophet.

But what does it say? So that he can perform miracles? God sends the spirit and power of Elijah so that he could raise the dead? No, it says so that he could turn the hearts of the fathers to the sons, and the sons to the fathers. Let me ask you as I have asked the Lord, "Why do we need the most powerful prophet to turn the hearts of the fathers to the sons? And the turn the hearts of the children to the fathers?" It's because in the last days, these two generations will be so much apart, it will be difficult to put them together.

What is happening to the Church all over the world? Young people are leaving the Church. Young people are getting disappointed with the Church, even though you may have a big church. Now, you might have a lot of young people in your church, but if you look at the national statistics, more and more young people are leaving the Church. That's why God sends Elijah.

In order to see how critical this is with regards to God's plan for the nations, let us examine two Bible case studies in 2 Kings, chapters 21 and 22. Consider the story of these two kings, both succeeding their fathers, who were the incumbent king. Two good kings, raised up two successors, but both turned out differently than their fathers.

BIBLICAL CASE STUDY #1

Manasseh becomes king of Israel, and he's only 12 years old. To be the king when you're only 12 years old is a very, very powerful stature. The Bible says that Manasseh became the most evil king of Israel. Manasseh was so evil that he sacrificed his own children to Baal, boiled them alive in boiling water. The Bible gives a commentary that there was no other king in Israel more evil than Manasseh.

Now, let me ask you a question. Where did Manasseh come from? He was the son of Hezekiah. And Hezekiah was a very good king. In fact, Hezekiah was one of those kings who really loved the Lord. So how can a very good king produce a very evil king? How can a king who loves the Lord produce the most evil king of Israel? Can an evil king come from a good King, who is his father? This is the consequence of the separation of the generations. **Hezekiah gave Manasseh freedom, but he did not prepare him for freedom.**

BIBLICAL CASE STUDY #2

There's another story in 2 Kings 22. Now here Josiah becomes king. He was 8 years old when he became king. He was a very good king. In fact, he reformed all of Israel. Restored worship at the temple. But the next king, Josiah's son, again, became a very evil king. Hezekiah's mistake was the same mistake Josiah committed. **They gave freedom to their children, but they never prepared them for freedom.**

Today's generation is making the same mistakes.

"The Test of a Civilization is what we do with our children"
Ravi Zacharias.

We all want revival, amen? Now, we're praying for revival in our nations, but are we preparing the next generation for revival? If not, it will be the same mistake that Hezekiah and Josiah committed. I believe God is actively participating in the preparation for revival as much as He is in the actual revival itself. He is preparing a generation of forerunners for the greatest revival the Church will ever see. Let us just work with God, not just in praying for revival, but more in preparing for that revival.

CURRENT HISTORY CASE STUDY #1

Let's look at our current history, the revival in Wales. 1904. This was the greatest revival the world has ever experienced. In a few days, hundreds and thousands of people came to the Lord. In 2004, there was a celebration of the revival's centennial in Wales. In the celebration, after 100 years of the revival, the Church has greatly diminished.

Why did this happen? We were not able to transfer the revival from one generation to the next. More than a hundred years ago, there was revival in the major continents of the world. And history shows that those revivals all ended up the same way Wales did. Maybe we have not learned to transfer revival to the next generation or we haven't learned to prepare the next generation for a true revival.

Just as Hezekiah and Josiah gave freedom to their sons but never prepared them for freedom, so have we given the blessings of revival to our children, but never prepared them to host these revivals.

If you are a student of revival, have you dug deep into its history and tried to discover why revival stopped, even when people have tasted it? You will find similar stories about people losing humility or giving in to pride. People lacked holiness, and people stopped being hungry for God.

CURRENT HISTORY CASE STUDY #2

I got saved in the Jesus People Movement in 1976. Some of you were not even born yet, though I still look younger than you. Jesus People Movement all over the world was just happening in every major city. After 10 years the movement died. During that time, the civil rights movement had started. Likewise, the Women's liberation movement gained momentum. The gay rights movement also began to grow. These movements are still alive today. So why is the Jesus Movement dead?

The main reason, I can think of, is that it was just one generation. The young people were not received by the older generation. During that time, the young people had long hair, wore t-shirts and jeans to church, took a bath once every two months, and came from a Hippie Culture. The Church rejected these extreme expressions of the youth, even when revival was happening among them. Because the movement was only a one-generation movement, it died very quickly.

I remember talking to a lady in Norway. Her son was 25 years old, and had been in his own apartment for two years. He never leaves the apartment, by himself. She said, "I don't know what he looks like. I've never seen him. He never leaves his house." When she brings him food, she puts it at the door, but she has to leave or he won't get the food. Even when you come to church, you can be in the midst of one thousand people and still feel alone. When a person is isolated, they go crazy.

As I have discussed in the previous chapter, if you isolate a church, the church dies. Isolation doesn't only kill a church, it can also kill a nation. But when it comes to generations, isolation can kill a revival, or it can kill the move of God. When a current generation is isolated from the previous, the work for God dies.

GOD DEFEATS ISOLATION THROUGH THE PRACTICE OF SUCCESSION IN SCRIPTURE

That's why it says, "I am the God of Abraham, Isaac, and Jacob." God seems to promote succession in the Scripture. If we don't learn to turn our hearts to the next generation, whatever God does in our generation dies with us.

I believe the number one strategy of Satan today is to isolate the generations. When he accomplishes that, he doesn't care if you have revival because we will never be able to pass it on to the next one. We can have all the miracles we want in our generation, even raise the dead or cross the Red Sea … but if we can't transfer them to the next generation because they are isolated, then it will not matter to Satan; he still wins in the end.

STRENGTHENING THE GENERATIONAL LINK BETWEEN THE GENERATIONS IS THE MAIN TASK OF THE SPIRIT AND POWER OF ELIJAH

Take a look at the example of Abraham, Isaac, and

Jacob. God speaks to Abraham. Abraham comes into the land as a foreigner. He does not own anything. He just had the word of the Lord. He passed the vision to Isaac. Isaac passed the vision to Jacob. And Jacob passes the vision to Joseph. This went to four generations, although he started as a foreigner with no land, no wealth, no property. Then He had Isaac, then Jacob, and then Joseph—four generations from Abraham. And Joseph becomes prime minister. Within just four generations Abraham's influence in the land went from Foreigner to Prime Minister. That describes an increase in influence, in power and jurisdiction.

I believe this is a very crucial truth that we have missed. If we learn to transfer God's vision and move from one generation to the next, or if we learn to transfer revival from one generation to the next, then if the biblical analogy is accurate in four generations, Christians will dominate culture and the influence in our nations. We must be experts in Generational Transfer.

This principle is seen in the Elijah and Elisha transfer. Elijah says, "I need to have a son. I'm the most powerful prophet, but the one coming next to me will be more powerful than I am." Finally, he finds Elisha, and he transfers the anointing to Elisha, and Elisha changes Israel. Elijah couldn't do it. He was so powerful, yet he couldn't do it. He had to transfer his anointing to the second generation—to Elisha. It was Elisha's anointing that killed Jezebel, totally changing the nation of Israel.

Another example of this is in the life of King David. All his life, he dreamt of building a temple. God didn't allow him. He needed a Solomon to build the temple. If you're a father or a mother, or just a part of the older generation and God gave you a dream for the Church or ministry, maybe it is to transfer that dream. If you feel like, "We're going to send thousands of missionaries all over the world or we're going to be a powerful church that impacts the government and the media and entertainment," is it possible that God has given you those dreams to transfer it to the next generation?

We get disappointed, discouraged, and frustrated. So we can't build the temple, just like David. Or we cannot change the nation like Elijah. Maybe God is just saying, "You need an Elisha, or you need a Solomon." Maybe the main reason we have "temples" unconstructed, or nations unchanged, is that we have not found our Elisha's or Solomon's to transfer these dreams.

In Joel 2:28, the prophecy goes,
"In the last days, I will pour out my spirit upon all flesh, you sons and daughters will prophesy, *you old men* shall dream dreams, and your *young men* shall see visions ..."

Notice that old men will have dreams, while the young will have visions. Is it possible that the reason young people today have no vision is because old men are not dreaming dreams anymore? We must dream again, for the sake of a visionless generation.

Chapter 20

THE 3 H CODE CAN BRING FORTH THE 3 R CHANGE

On the following page I've put a summary in a chart. You see the personal application is: **Don't drink any wine, don't cut your hair, and don't touch any dead body.** This is for your personal life. Then it becomes nationwide, "If my people will have **humility**, **hunger**, and **holiness**."

Humility will bring a revolution in a generation where everybody wants to be famous. "How many friends do you have on Facebook?" Or, "How many views do you have on your YouTube video?" The more famous you are, the more successful you are. The Bible says, "The meek shall inherit the earth." It's a different kind of revolution.

Hunger for God will bring revival. If we are really hungry for God, then it will bring revival. Yes, we are hungry for God. But we are hungrier for iPads. We are hungrier for movies. We have so many other hungers that our hunger for God is so small compared to them. Let me ask you a question.

What if we gathered all the churches in your city? The big churches and small churches. The young churches and the old churches. All the churches—conservative and liberal. If we gathered all of them, and in one day they cried out to God to come, "Would God come? Yes, He will. Because when all the churches come together there is unity.

Question: So, why don't we do it? Why don't we gather the churches together, especially if we know it would bring God down?

Answer: **We are not hungry enough.** If we are hungry enough, we will bring God down. Hunger for God will bring revival.

How about **the holiness of God?** It will reform our nations. Why would a doctor abort a baby? Not because the law says yes. He can still make a choice. If he has a conscience, if people would have consciences today, they will do good. **Holiness will restore the conscience to society.**

Just take a look at the Nazarite lifestyle. If this generation will be a humble generation, they will bring a revolution. If this generation will be hungry for God, they will bring revival. If this generation is a holy generation, they will reform our nations.

Why are we doing the Nazarite training? Because we want the next generation to live a lifestyle of humility, holiness, and hunger.

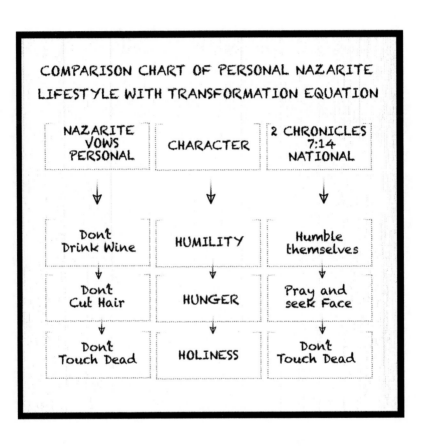

COMPARISON CHART OF PERSONAL NAZARITE LIFESTYLE WITH TRANSFORMATION EQUATION

NAZARITE VOWS PERSONAL	CHARACTER	2 CHRONICLES 7:14 NATIONAL
Don't Drink Wine	HUMILITY	Humble themselves
Don't Cut Hair	HUNGER	Pray and seek Face
Don't Touch Dead	HOLINESS	Don't Touch Dead

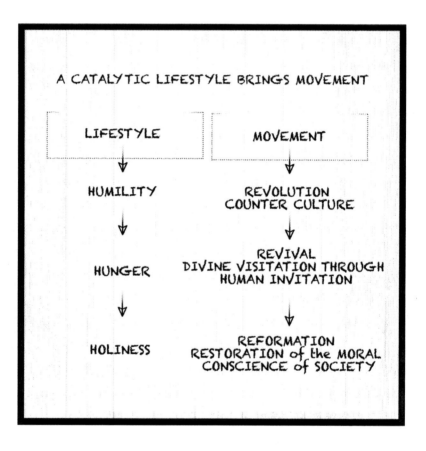

A CATALYTIC LIFESTYLE BRINGS MOVEMENT

LIFESTYLE	MOVEMENT
HUMILITY	REVOLUTION COUNTER CULTURE
HUNGER	REVIVAL DIVINE VISITATION THROUGH HUMAN INVITATION
HOLINESS	REFORMATION RESTORATION of the MORAL CONSCIENCE of SOCIETY

PART 4

THE CHOICE

The Blind Nazarite or the RAPTURED Nazarite,
the choice this generation has to make.

Chapter 21

WEAPONS OF MASS DISTRACTION (WMD)

Ironically, the presence of an anointed Nazarite does not assure victory in bringing transformation in a nation. The potential is there, but the enemy breaks in with a massive bombardment of distractions ... I call the WMD's.

These weapons are so effective, though the forms may change throughout the ages, but the results are almost the same.

The Samson Syndrome is the typical attack Satan uses when he focuses on the outside form of one's lifestyle, which totally defeats the person or renders them ineffective. In Samson's case, the length of his hair wasn't really the true source of his power, but his covenant with God expressed through the length of his hair.

Satan distracted him in all fronts of his covenant. He violated his vows by drinking, playing with women and disrespecting what he stood for by cutting his hair. He was unconscious when his hair was cut. In fact, his spirit was so distracted that he didn't even know that the Spirit of God had already left him after his hair was cut. He apparently didn't feel the departure of strength, as he still tried to feel himself, but could not.

Just like today, many couldn't even recognize the "Ichabod", the departure of God's glory and presence, simply because the focus has been on one's pride of achievements and abilities, rather than their dependence on God's promise to fulfill His covenant with them.

Today Satan has unleashed his Weapons of Mass Distraction (WMD), carried by the present technology. It is actually the same distractions Samson faced, but this time on steroids. The WMD of Social Media, highlighting and accelerating discontent through comparisons. It's so easy to change one's countenance from enjoying their day into total dismay—all they have to do is open their Facebook and see how their friends are doing, especially if they're doing a lot better than they are.

What killed Samson wasn't another mighty man, but a simple distraction that changed his focus from his sense of destiny, highlighted by his Nazarite vows since birth which separated him for God's purpose, into his temporary pleasures. What a scheme of things!

Today, Satan has the power of Media, which is accessible 24/7, to deliver those distractions into our very bedrooms.

IF SATAN CAN DISTRACT YOU,
HE CAN DESTROY YOU.

Chapter 22

INTENTIONAL OR ACCIDENTAL

On the other hand, there was another story of an Ancient Nazarite called Elijah. Although he wasn't labeled a Nazarite like Samson was, a careful examination of his life and his commitment points to it.

When John The Baptist in the New Testament was referred to as the "Elijah" that has come, we should notice that he had a peculiar diet, locusts and honey … a reference to a unique lifestyle that is commonly associated with Nazarites.

There are many similarities with Samson and Elijah. Both of them have extra ordinary supernatural gifts. Samson had supernatural strength, while Elijah had a supernatural ability to call fire from Heaven or even perform unusual miracles.

Aside from that, both of them carried National prominent positions. Samson was appointed to be a judge over Israel, since Israel didn't have a king at that time. Elijah, was appointed as a prophet to the nation of Israel when Kings started to rule. We would probably refer to him as the highest religious leader of the nation, as prophets at that time played an important role in national affairs.

A third similarity was their failures or setbacks they experienced with women. Samson was deceived by Delilah to reveal his sacred vow to not cut his hair; therefore, exposing himself to the vulnerability of the enemy. Elijah was a local idol at that time. He had cleansed the nation of 800 prophets of Baal in his Mt. Carmel encounter, and yet, he was overcome by fear from a woman, Jezebel, the wife of Ahab the King of Israel. In his fear, Elijah hid in a cave, wanting to die.

When we further examine the stories, we find out where Samson failed and Elijah succeeded. This is not because one was better than the other, because they lived in totally different environments. But we discover that Samson was so spiritually blinded that he lost sight of the bigger picture, or his purpose and destiny. He was called to defeat the Philistines. "Hey, what's the purpose of his strength anyway? To just win muscle contests or simple entertainment?" When you are in the middle of being distracted, you make dumb decisions. You become blind to your own future. This is what Samson experienced.

Elijah on the other hand, called on God inside the cave. The earthquake came, the wind that shattered the rocks came, (that must have been a category 5 hurricane) and the fire that usually signifies God's presence—all to completely silence Elijah. I imagine that after all that violent, noisy and chaotic background, there came an absolute silence.

Even Elijah's thoughts were grounded. He was dumbfounded. In that backdrop a still small voice came to him. Then sudden silence got his total, absolute attention. He heard every word, paid attention to every intonation, listened intently to the whole whisper. For why does one whisper except to make sure only one person hears—it was for "his ears only."

Elijah intentionally focused on his future destiny. He needed to transfer his mantle to the next generation, Elisha. This differentiated him from Samson, who died with no successor. Although Samson was honored among the men of faith, as he was able to kill more of his enemies in his death than in his life, his work still ended with his death. While Elijah's work and anointing continued in a double portion in Elisha's life. What a story! What a contrast!

Today's generation can look at this contrast and say that's nice. Or they can open their eyes and see that they face a choice today. They can either chose the path of Samson or the path of Elijah. Yes, one can be a Nazarite, yet which kind will you be? One can also ask similarly, what kind of a disciple of Jesus will you be? One that follows Him to the end or one who would sell Him for 30 pieces of silver?

Every young person who loves Jesus will have to face the unavoidable choice—will you? There are many Samson's in this young generation. A gifted, talented and anointed young generation, yet once distracted, they lose sight of their destiny. Many young, pop singers today, started as choir members in the church, discovering and enhancing their singing abilities in church events and celebrations. Now, many of them have lost sight of their destiny, forgetting the very values that they should stand for. Popularity, just like prosperity, can be a powerful distraction.

I have seen lives of emerging and promising, powerful young leaders who have been totally destroyed because of veering away from their destinies. Some fall like Samson to women, while others simply lose their humility. Worldly success can be blinding.

This has happened so many times that we tend to think success in the world is incompatible with Kingdom success. I beg to disagree. I believe that one can be successful in the entertainment business or in the marketplace and still remain on fire for God. One can be a billionaire and still be humble before Him. Abraham did it; David did it; Job did it—so can we.

Samson failed at his distraction, but Elijah didn't. He sought out for a successor. When the time came, God raptured Elijah into the heavens with chariots. Maybe God knew that if Elijah stayed any longer, he would have been distracted, too. But nonetheless, Elijah is out of the picture and Elisha is on stage. Elisha picks up Elijah's mantle and went on to perform more miracles than his predecessor. What a picture. What an object lesson.

This is what real success in the Kingdom of God is. It is not how many Philistines or enemies you have defeated; it is whether you have successfully transferred your anointing or mantle to the next anointed generation of leaders. If not, then no matter what you have done in your generation, it will all be lost in the next one.

Elijah was so successful in his work that God kept on using him for the end time message.

Chapter 23

UNFOLDING THE THREEFOLD DIMENSION OF THE ELIJAH MANTLE/MANDATE

It is imperative that we understand what the Scriptures meant when it talks about the spirit of Elijah. What anointing did Elijah carry? Why was John the Baptist synonymously associated with the power of Elijah? Did Jesus just talk about John when He spoke of Elijah? Or is there another Elijah that is to come?

These are just a handful of questions that come to mind when we consider the spirit and power of Elijah. Most of which, could be answered theologically. But when we consider the young generation today, we must better answer these questions, prophetically. There is a mystery about Elijah's mantle that we could examine. Maybe we can find answers by looking closely at what the Scriptures say about him. It could be a crucial key in raising up the next generation.

There are three mentions of Elijah in the Bible as it relates to the end times. Jesus mentions the two times Elijah will come after the first Elijah,

> "And the disciples asked him, 'Then why do the scribes say that first Elijah must come?' He

answered, 'Elijah does come, and **he will restore all things**. **But I tell you that Elijah has already come**, and they did not recognize him, but did to him whatever they pleased. So also the Son of Man will certainly suffer at their hands.' Then the disciples understood that he was speaking to them of John the Baptist" (Mathew 17:10-13).

This means that there are 3 Elijah's. I believe it represents three dimensions of Elijah's mantle of anointing. Let us examine the three Elijah's of the bible.

THE ANOINTING

The first Elijah was the Tishbite. **His name in the Hebrew means, literally, "My God is Yahweh," (1 Kings 17:1).**

Elijah displayed an extraordinary anointing in the Old Testament. He was arguably the most powerful prophet who ever lived. He came at a time when Israel was in a deep spiritual crisis, and God raised him up as a prophetic voice. At one point in his life, he was able to call down fire from Heaven at will, and eventually, he was taken from this world by fire itself.

Elijah's anointing was in a class of its own. A prophet of his caliber (in terms of signs and wonders) we never see again in the Bible. We can say that his only protégé, Elisha, was probably more powerful, but we can still trace where it all came from—Elijah.

Although Elisha, had a double portion of his anointing, Elijah's experiences were unique and exclusive to himself. From the showdown against the false prophets at Mt. Carmel, to hearing that "still small voice" at Mt. Horeb, Elijah's journey is, no doubt, one of the stories we follow when we talk about anointing. The astonishing display of God's power is undeniably unparalleled in the life of this prophet.

THE MESSAGE
John the Baptist (Second Elijah), Luke 1:17

Elijah's message was of repentance and reformation. We see this marked in the life of John the Baptist, whose sole mandate was to prepare the way of the Lord, the first coming of the Messiah. Jesus Himself mentions to His disciples that John was the Elijah that everyone was waiting for.

However, notice the irony of the spirit of Elijah upon the life of John the Baptist. He possessed the anointing described as the most powerful in history, and yet, he did not perform one single miracle. Instead, like Elijah, he was a prophetic voice raised up by God to address the generation of that time. John himself, described his ministry as "a voice." He may not have performed one single miracle, but he raised up a dead generation. He was the one who introduced Jesus as the Bridegroom, which later leads to the revelation of the Church, the Bride. He made ready a people for the coming of the Messiah. Apparently, a feat only made possible with the spirit and power of Elijah.

THE RESPONSIBILITY

The Third Elijah could refer to a whole generation, instead of one person," (Matthew 17:11).

When we consider the present day that we live in, aren't we in need of the same anointing today? Previously, we looked at the nightmares of this generation. Doesn't the spirit of Elijah play a major role in breaking the curse and attack upon this generation? We know about the anointing; we know about the message; now this leads us to the responsibility that goes with the spirit of Elijah.

Malachi 4:5-6 describes sending the prophet Elijah. In this passage, Elijah is sent for one single purpose,

"… To turn the hearts of the fathers to the children, and the hearts of the children to the fathers."

Look at the generations today; look at the families; and look at the churches. Broken homes, broken congregations, and broken relationships. Is it possible that Malachi was prophesying another Elijah who is to come, and Jesus affirming his responsibility to "restore all things?"

Why do we need the spirit of Elijah today?

Because we need its three-sided mantle: the anointing, the message and the purposefulness of the most powerful prophet to restore all things. We need the supernatural anointing for signs and wonder. This will surely capture the minds of this young generation who have not seen, only heard of God's miracles.

We need the message of intimacy with God, which was spoken by John the Baptist. He was the first to ever speak of God as a Bridegroom. His passion for truth and righteousness can only come from a deep love for God. This speaks against the "casualness" of the relationship our generation has toward God.

God has been reduced to a commodity and church is a mere option. The message of John will break open the blinding veil over this generation and wake them up to the fruit of holiness that can only come from real intimacy.

Finally we need to highlight the Need to RESTORE ALL THINGS. Before there is a need to restore all things, then all things must first be lost.

We seemed to have lost influence in every major sphere of society. There was once upon a time when Christians took the lead, even in science, in government, the arts, both literary and performing arts and education. This is not true today. We have not only lost our strong influence, but we are losing our young generation fast. Somehow, we are losing the ability to INSPIRE them to be involved with Church and missions. This is why we need the spirit of Elijah.

But in order to fulfill the vision of restoring all things, because of the amount of spiritual corrosion that has taken place, we would need the complete mantle of the spirit of Elijah, including the Anointing and the Message of intimacy.

I think we are not looking for one man in the end times to stand as Elijah. I believe God has prepared a whole generation to do it. Bishop Bill Hammon called it the Saints Movement, others have called it Joel's Army. Regardless of what they are called, this Elijah Generation will have to take the responsibility to restore all things.

PART 5

THE EPIC BATTLE

You only meet Goliaths at the DMZ.

It was on July 29, 2016, a Friday in Seoul, Korea. We woke up early in the morning to prepare for the most intense gathering I have ever organized in my life. This is the UPRISING 2016 Korea, where we have called young leaders from all over the world to gather at the DMZ (Demilitarized Zone) between North and South Korea, the border. Some people would call it the no man's land or the battle line.

We had been meeting for three days at the Ilsan Kwanglin Church, getting our hearts ready and our spirits in tune before we all went to the border to join several Young South Koreans to fast and pray and confront the Goliath of Division that has taunted the South Korean churches for decades.

We believed that the young generation, powerful as the David's of today, needed to see the Goliath's taunting the Church, so that they will wake up to their DNA. Oh yes, UPRISING is not just another conference. It is a call to the Battle line, a call to confront the Goliath-sized issues that face the young generations today.

When David saw Goliath for the first time, his blood started to boil. He couldn't accept the reality he was facing. Content to pastor sheep in the desert, he felt a slap in the face. The Bible says, "David heard him (Goliath)." When every Israelite soldier was afraid, David wasn't. All he could feel were the UNACCEPTABLE insults, this 'uncircumcised Philistine' was shouting. When he was questioned by his brother Eliab about his intentions, David said the famous quote we always hear:

"And David said, 'What have I now done? Is there not a cause?'" (1 Samuel 17:29).

That was what we were aiming for—a generation of young David's who were waking up to the Cause to fight. A challenge as big as Goliath that would slap them in the face to wake up to the reality of their destiny—slaying these giants.

As we woke up to that final day, we were intimidated by the weather. The Acu-weather forecast was "multiple thunderstorms." They forecasted an hourly thunderstorm at the Paju city, where the border is. It was dark, wet and raining. Thinking about cancelling the DMZ gathering was on our mind. It might be the safest thing to do for more than a thousand young leaders who were coming from more than 37 nations.

After much consideration, we decided to continue with the gathering. Only when lightning is present will we shut down the event. What if we had to close down … all these people had traveled, paid for their way and now faced a possible cancelation? All these questions ran through my mind.

Then, I heard God whisper to me, "Well, what do you expect at the border? A tour or a battle?" I realized that I was chickening out. So decisively, I said … "Rain or shine we go."

When we arrived at the border three hours earlier, we found the place dry and absolutely no rain, just some cloud covering. God's affirmation was so sweet and assurance of victory so certain.

We spent seven hours at the border, worshiping, praying, fasting, crying out and defying the Goliath of Division between

North and South Korea. We confronted the Goliaths facing this generation—the Attacks representing the Goliaths taunting the Church are abortion, child trafficking, teen-age suicide, immorality, family breakdown, child soldiers and the massive distraction among the youth.

We ended with an amazing candle lighting time where these lights multiplied as one lighted each other's candle. It was symbolic, prophetic and a reminder for all those who participated. Let His light shine—not ours.

We went back to our hotels refreshed and greatly fired up, knowing that God led us to the border, the DMZ.

I believe we have a generation who is sleeping on their potential to confront the Goliaths of the Church or the Kingdom. The best way to describe this generation is UNDER CHALLENGED.

When we see our young people finding more challenges on video games than in the mission fields, then they are under challenged. When we see them sneaking out of our worship services to stand outside our sanctuaries, they are under challenged. When we have to bribe them to come to our youth groups, youth outreaches, then we are under challenging them. They need to see and face the Goliath that is destroying their generation. Then they will wake up and say with David, "Is there not a cause?"

The problem is, you only see Goliath's at the DMZ, the border, the battle line, the battle field. Psalms 110:3 says,

"On the day you fight your enemies, your people

will volunteer. Like the dew of early morning your young men will come to you on the sacred hills."

If you are a young person reading this book, you are more than what the world describes you to be. I have a very high respect for this young generation, because I know they will change the world. Satan wants to destroy you because he is afraid of you.

You don't have to be a prophet to see what Satan is doing. You know what Satan is doing? He is killing the children before they reach their full maturity. And every time you see in the Bible where Satan kills children, it is because he is afraid.

He was afraid of Moses, so he killed the children. He was afraid of Jesus, so he killed the children. Now, he's doing this all over the world. Why is Satan killing the children all over the world? I believe it's because Satan knows that a generation is coming that will change the world! Yes, he is aware that this generation is so powerful that he has to stop this generation before they are born.

I say this to young people all over the world. If you're alive today, and you're a young person, you're a survivor. Why did God choose you to survive? Because God knows you will change the world.

It is time to wake up the sleeping Davids because the Goliaths are proliferating!

Chapter 24

THE 7 MOUNTAINS TO OCCUPY OR ARE THEY 7 MOUNT CARMEL CONFRONTATIONS?

I want to say to all the young people, "Satan doesn't want to hurt you; he wants to kill you. He's not killed you yet because he's not reached you yet. But you know why he wants to kill you? Because he's afraid of you."

I believe in raising up a generation of forerunners. These forerunners will not just occupy the 7 mountains of culture, but rather fight the 7 Mount Carmel confrontations in the Kingdom.

Why again do I believe this so much? It is not just a bunch of religious clichés that I stand on. Let us review the reality.

This generation is not only global, it is the most prophesied generation in the history of the Church. Try to go to all the conferences all over the world. Always, you will hear people say, "There will be a generation that will bring in the biggest harvest the world has ever seen. There will be a generation that will transform cities all over the world. There will be a powerful generation coming that will shift the destiny of nations."

Bill Bright said it. Loren Cunningham said it. Denominational leaders prophesied it. This generation is the most prophesied generation in history of the Church.

This generation thinks digital—thinks very fast. When I buy a computer, I read the manual. You know, page by page, how does it work? You know how young people buy a computer today? They plug it in and turn it on. You know why? Because they live in the context of a digital environment where they are comfortable with computers.

You've probably heard me say it, but my generation is the Polaroid generation. Remember when you needed to take a picture to a company and have it developed—for a week? Only after one week you find out the results of your pictures, "Oh, they are all terrible shots, all 36 of them!" If you remember that, then you're as old as I am.

How the Polaroid work so vividly describes how we in the older generation work. You take a picture and a paper comes out. And slowly the picture develops. That's how the older generation thinks.

If you offer a suggestion to a group of old people, they will say, "Can I think about it for one week?" After one week, "Let's form a committee to think about it for another week." After two weeks, "Let's study it further for another week." After three weeks, if we can still remember the suggestion, then we can make a decision.

This generation is so different because they think digital. A Digital generation produced a digital perception. You take a picture, and the picture is right there. They make a decision, save or delete, and that's how fast this generation thinks. Have you ever watched an MTV program? Hundreds of pictures are flashed in just one song. One MTV song takes a long time to produce. We see a generation that has been trained to think and process information very fast.

Most young people when asked by their parents if they could teach them how to start a Facebook page, will just say, "Dad, Mom, I'll just do it for you. It is too complicated." It is not that they are wiser; it is just that they are so used to it, they think faster. They are wired that way.

Once more, I mentioned that this generation has **NO VOLUME CONTROL.** When my son listens to his iPod on his earphones, he is wearing the earphones, but I can still hear the music. I said, "Son, you don't understand what low volume is?" For most young people, if it's not loud, it's not music. Digital takes away the volume control.

It reflects the way they think. **It's either you're in, or you're out. It's either I'm involved, or not involved.** There's no gradually getting involved. That's why this generation is very special. **This is the only generation that can carry a message that is tailor-made for them—a message of NO COMPROMISE** and holiness unto God. It's in their DNA.

When we talk about occupying the 7 mountains of culture, I believe in the final reality; it will not be occupation, but confrontations. The Goliaths who occupy those mountains of influence won't just give up their territory. Only a Mount Carmel confrontation will restore those mountains of influence to the Church.

I am not promoting Dominion Theology here. I am describing what is inevitable. When an Elijah Generation restores all things, it will be a battle; yes, but it will be a spiritual one. Nazarites, who display humility, pursue holiness and cultivate hunger for God will bring a counter culture revolution, a moral reformation and a spiritual revival.

Giants will fall. Influence will be restored to the Church. Nations will be changed. But it will be done without worldly weapons of aggression, hostility and manipulation.

This will be accomplished by being 2 Chronicles 7:14, "If my people, who are called by my name will humble themselves, pray and seek my face, turn from their wicked ways. Then, I will hear from heaven, forgive their sins and heal their land."

Chapter 25

THE NEXT JESUS PEOPLE MOVEMENT IS THE DIGITAL NAZARITE MOVEMENT

I believe that the next Jesus People Movement will be different from the previous one. It will be different in that this coming movement will not physically separate themselves from the world through communes or subcultures. This describes the movement where I got saved. We wanted to build communes to separate ourselves from the worldly institutions and be ourselves. We had a saying then, "You can't change something that you are a part of."

The coming movement won't change the world from the outside, but from the inside. The problem is not the capacity, but the challenge.

You know how old the youngest suicide bomber was that they caught in Israel? He was eight years old. He strapped a bomb around his waist. It did not explode, so he was caught— an 8-year-old suicide bomber.

Do you know that in other religions, they train children as young as five to six years old to be suicide bombers? What do we do with our five year olds? We babysit them in church. What do we do with our young people? "Oh, come to church once a week. Just come to church once a week. If you don't want to come, we'll give you pizza so you will come."

As I have previously said in this book over and over again, this is the most under challenged generation in the history of the Church. If a generation can do a lot, but the challenge we present to them is so low, they won't come. We can say, "Oh, just come to church once a week. That's Christianity—just come to church once a week." They'll get frustrated. And what will they say in church? "We're bored with church."

If they can actually be nation-changers, and we only call them to a minimum commitment, "Come to church once a week," then because our challenge is too low it will result in frustration and a lack of interest.

Today, an extreme religious order is challenging young people to fight in Syria a war that they don't fully understand, using weapons that they barely know how to use and in a place where they have no reason to fight. Then, why are they coming to Syria to fight? They are drawn by the challenge. The level of challenge brings them respect. They don't feel marginalized or taken for granted. I agree that some of this is just pure naivety or plain gullibility.

This is precisely the reason why Jesus Revolution started a Nazarite Training. If we don't become experts in transferring what God is doing in our generation to the next, we will lose this generation. If we don't release this generation to their destiny, they will self-destruct.

There's a verse in Amos 2:12-13, where God says:
"But you made the Nazirites drink wine, And you

commanded the prophets saying, 'You shall not prophesy! Behold, I am weighted down beneath you ...'"

The Message Bible puts it this way:
"But you made the youth–in–training break training ...You're too much for me. I'm hard–pressed—to the breaking point."

God was angry over Israel because they made their Nazarites drink wine. You see Nazarites in the Old Testament are very powerful men and women. They are committed 100 percent to God. When they make this consecration to be a Nazarite, all of Israel watches their lives as a standard.

In Amos 2:12, God gets angry at Israel because they made the Nazarites drink wine. This simply means that they made the Nazarites violate their own extreme devotion.

I think this is what's happening in this generation. We have a generation that can be on fire for God. A generation that can be 100 percent committed to the Lord, but is it like making the Nazarites drink wine, when we stop this generation from becoming extreme for God?

"Oh don't read the Bible too much. Oh, don't commit too much on the ministry or missions. Oh, church is just like this." Instead, when young people can die for what they believe in. This generation is very different from us. If we want to save them, we need to challenge them.

Let me close with just 2 stories.

I have a friend in Germany, who got so on fire for God; he's 29 years old. He organized The Call Berlin—it's a gathering to fast and pray for Germany. I mean he is so good; although, he had no experience in gathering people. On a special day, he gathered three German speaking countries— Austria, Switzerland, and Germany. Thousands of young people came together. There was a different atmosphere.

We prayed the last night before the gathering at a cathedral in Berlin. As the worship team led worship, all of a sudden somebody blew the shofar—a ram's horn. I witnessed 800 young people scream at the top of their voices. They were screaming so loudly that you couldn't hear the worship team. And you know what they were screaming? We thought they were just excited for the following day. But they were screaming this: "Lord, give us Germany! Lord, turn Germany back to You! Germany belongs to the next generation!"

They were screaming so loudly and it lasted for thirty minutes. The worship team had to stop. Everybody knelt down and started to weep. Then, all of a sudden, there was silence. Even the children present were quiet. For thirty minutes, there was screaming, then afterwards just dead silence. It's like God walked into the room.

My friend, Walter Heidenreich, who has been one of the National leaders in Germany, was kneeling down with us. He whispered to me, "Jerome, what do you think happened?"

I said, "I could only describe it like a dam bursting and the water coming out."

My friend said, "Do you know today is the 70th anniversary since Hitler came into power. It was like the cry and the voice of a generation was silenced for 70 years and was suddenly released today." It was very powerful.

The event was powerful. My friend started a holy revolution school in Hanover, Germany. Young people are extreme for God. After two years, my friend was accused of domestic violence. Police came to his house, arrested him, and took him to jail. It became a nationwide scandal. After several months of investigation, he was found innocent, but it destroyed the entire ministry that he had because his marriage never worked.

There's another story in Australia. This guy was a worship leader. You probably know the song, "The Healer." It was #2 on the Hillsong Gospel charts for several years. This guy was only 25 years old. He was very gifted and very anointed. But every time he sang, he pulled an oxygen tank. He had oxygen hoses attached to his nose because he says he's dying of cancer. When they sang his song, "The Healer," everybody would weep and cry—praying for his healing.

Then, in 2008, he was interviewed live on the Cable News network BBC, and confessed that it was a lie. He wasn't sick. He deceived his parents, raised hundreds of thousands of dollars for his medication, but he wasn't sick of cancer.

His father was a pastor in Adelaide, Australia, and declared, "I'll return all the money that you've sent to my son." When he was asked, "Why did you do it? Why did you lie?" he said on international television, "See, I was really addicted to pornography. Every time someone asked me how I was doing, I felt bad saying that, "I'm doing fine. So I invented a sickness so that people would pray for me."

I don't condemn our brothers who have fallen. It can happen to anyone of us. I mention them with deep respect and understanding, believing that God will restore them as they continue to serve God. We have a generation that is very gifted and very talented, but if we don't raise them up to be humble, holy, and hungry for God, their ministry will die. They will be like Samson or they will self-destruct.

The three powerful codes of a Nazarite are the keys to Revival, Reformation and Revolution. These codes are: Humility, Holiness and Hunger.

These three things are so powerful that they can carry your gifts and your anointing. In one of my wedding anniversaries, I bought my wife a diamond ring. They say if you give your wife a diamond ring, it's a gift for life. I thought that it was such a great idea; and then I won't have to buy her a gift ever again. I found out later that this is not true.

When she looked at it, she said, "Wow, beautiful. Where is it?"

I said, "It's there. It's so small, but it's there. Believe me by faith it's there." I couldn't afford the big one.

When I saw this ring with a big diamond in the jewelry store, worth $20,000, it had, interestingly, three prongs or three clamps holding the diamond in place. Only three clamps hold it. If you're a jeweler, you'll make sure those clamps are really strong. If one of those clamps breaks, you'll lose $20,000.

I look at the diamond as your gifts, your abilities, and your talents. It's what God can do in your life. If you don't have **humility, holiness, and hunger**, you can lose your potential. They are like the three clamps that hold your value. If they break, you will lose what God has given you.

I leave you with a warning and a hope. I pray that the commentary on the book of Judges will not be a description of our generation.

> "… and there arose another generation after them
> who did not know the Lord, nor yet the work
> which He had done for Israel" (Judges 2:10)

If we don't make our ministry to the next generation our priority, someone in the future might end up describing our sons and daughter with these comments.

Rather, if we receive the Spirit and Power of Elijah and prepare the next generation to be bold and courageous, I pray they will be described by this verse.

> "And they have conquered him by the blood of
> the Lamb and by the word of their testimony,
> for they loved not their lives even unto death"
> (Revelation 12:11).

May God raise up a Generation of Nazarites who carry the spirit and power of Elijah!

ABOUT THE AUTHOR

Jerome Ocampo has been in ministry for 32 years. Currently he is the Senior Pastor and Co-Founder of *Jesus' Flock Gateway Church* in the Philippines. He also founded the prayer movement called *Jesus Revolution Now* and spear-headed the global youth convergence called *UPRISING (United Prayer Rising)*.

With the burning vision to prepare and raise the next generation of leaders, he has preached around the world about the true essence of the *Nazarite* call—a call that has marked this generation to be a significant voice in every sphere of society. He has already conducted trainings around the world, especially in East Asia, Australia, Europe, and the United States, producing three manuals to help with the teaching.

He lives in Manila with his wife, Annabelle (Abel), and their three sons, Paul, Johan, and Jemuel, all of whom are serving full-time in the ministry.

For more information, or to schedule and conduct the Nazarite Training in your church, or have Rev. Ocampo speak at your conference, contact him at:

www.jesusrev.com
info@jesusrev.com